Out of the Wilderness

*_God's Path to Glory_*

Pastor Paulin Kamuangu

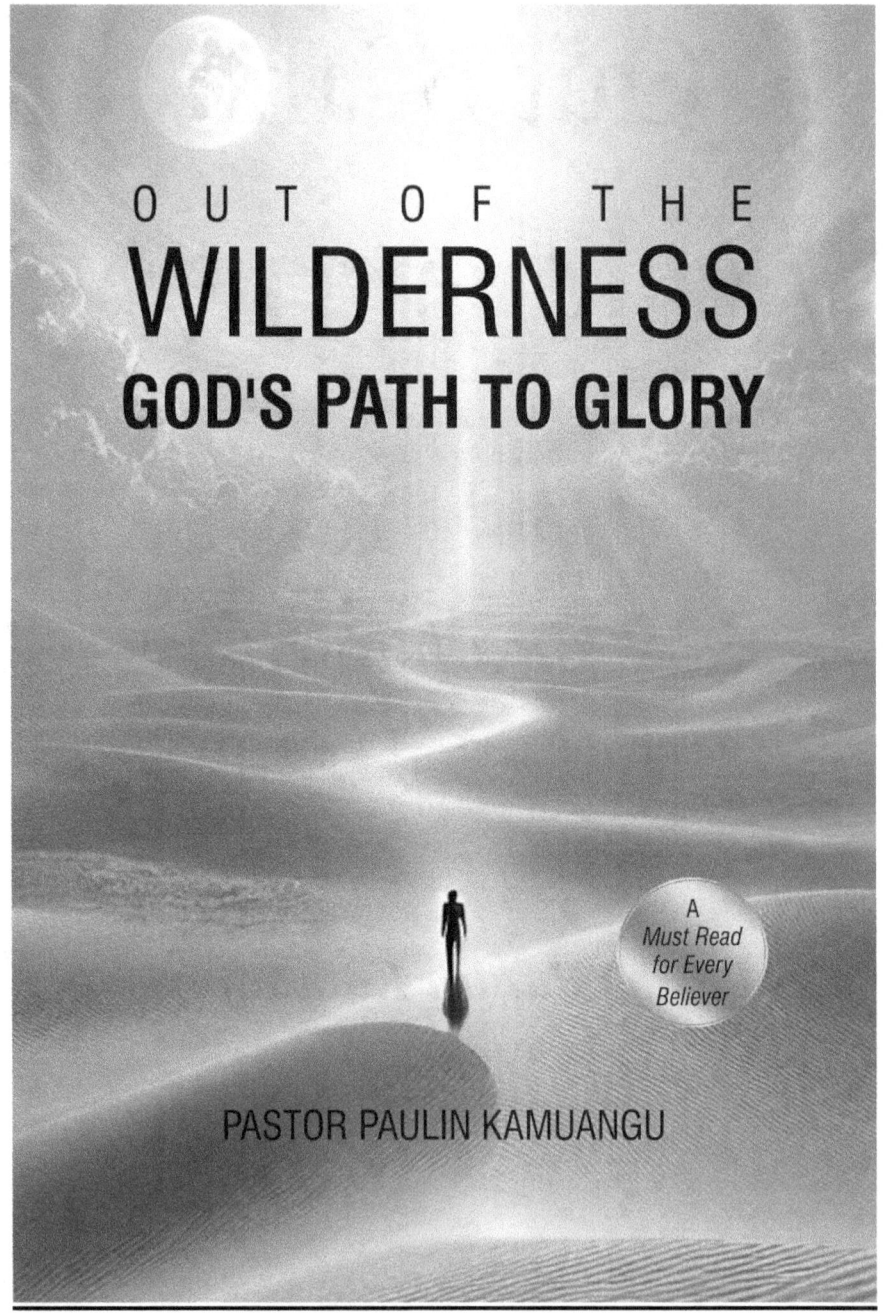

Copyright Notice

Unless otherwise indicated, all Scripture quotations are taken from the King James Version, New International Version, and New International Version.

Out of the Wilderness: God's Path to Glory

ISBN: 979-8-9923499-0-0

©2025, Rev. Paulin Kamuangu

Published by Spirit Chapel Ministries

For personal copies of this book, information about other books, or bulk purchases, please contact:

Tel: +1 (617) 784-5073

Email: kamuangu@gmail.com

All Rights Reserved

No part of this book may be reproduced, written, electronic, recorded, or photocopied without written permission from the publisher or author.

The exception would be in the case of brief quotations embodied in critical articles or reviews and pages where permission is specifically granted by the publisher or author.

TABLE OF CONTENTS

Preface _____ 5

Acknowledgment _____ 7

Dedication _____ 9

Introduction _____ 11

Chapter One _____ 19

    Understanding the Wilderness _____ 19

    The Wilderness is Not the End _____ 25

    The Wilderness is a Season, Not a Destination _____ 27

    Waiting for God's Timing _____ 31

    Grace in the Wilderness _____ 37

    The Nature of Grace in the Wilderness _____ 40

    Practical Steps to Embrace Grace in the Wilderness _____ 41

Chapter Two _____ 43

    Navigating the Wilderness Experience with the Inner Man _____ 43

    The Strength of the Inner Man _____ 54

    The Role of Spiritual Strength _____ 55

    Walking in Obedience to God's Word _____ 62

Chapter Three _____ 69

    The Training in the Wilderness _____ 69

Chapter Four _____ 81

    The Temptation and Trial in the Wilderness _____ 81

    Proclaiming Victory and Restoration _____ 96
Chapter Five _____ *103*
    The Experience of the Promised Land _____ 103
    The Promise of Renewal _____ 109
    Renewal through God's Word_____ 110
    Walking in the Promise of Renewal _____ 113
    Walking in Divine Victory _____ 115
Reflective Questions and Group Discussion Prompts _____ *123*
*Conclusion*_____ *127*

PREFACE

The journey of life is often filled with seasons of challenge, growth, and transformation. As believers, these experiences are not random but divinely orchestrated to shape us into vessels of God's glory. In Scripture, the wilderness is a recurring theme—a place of testing, refining, and preparation. It is not a destination but a pathway to the Promised Land. This book, *Out of the Wilderness: God's Path to Glory*, seeks to unpack the profound spiritual truths hidden in the wilderness experience and guide believers on their own transformative journeys.

As the Senior Pastor of **Spirit Chapel Ministries** in the United States, I have been privileged to shepherd countless individuals through their wilderness seasons. In my years of ministry, I have witnessed how God uses trials, temptations, and challenges to strip away self-will and replace it with His divine purpose. The wilderness is not a place of defeat; it is a place of divine encounter where the Spirit of God refines us for greater glory.

This book is inspired by the countless testimonies of those who have emerged from their wilderness seasons with renewed faith, strength, and clarity of purpose. Drawing from Biblical narratives, practical examples, and timeless spiritual principles, *Out of the Wilderness* aims to provide insight, encouragement, and hope for anyone navigating the wilderness of life.

Whether you are facing trials that test your faith, seasons of waiting that stretch your patience, or temptations that challenge your obedience, this book is for you. It is my prayer that through these pages, you will discover the beauty of God's design in your wilderness and embrace the transformation that leads to His glory.

LET US JOURNEY TOGETHER through the wilderness, trusting that God's plan for us is not to harm but to prosper, not to leave us stranded but to bring us into His promises. May the lessons and revelations in this book inspire you to trust in God's process, hold on to His promises, and step into the fullness of His glory.

Blessings,

Rev. Paulin Kamuangu
G.O & Senior Pastor,

Spirit Chapel Ministries

Acknowledgment

Writing *Out of the Wilderness: God's Path to Glory* has been a deeply transformative journey, one that would not have been possible without the support, encouragement, and inspiration of many individuals. I am profoundly grateful to God, whose guidance, wisdom, and grace have been the cornerstone of this work. Every revelation in this book is a testament to His faithfulness and unfailing love.

To my loving family, your unwavering support has been my greatest blessing. To my wife and children, thank you for your patience, prayers, and encouragement as I dedicated countless hours to writing and ministry. Your love fuels my passion to serve and inspire others.

To the Spirit Chapel Ministries family, you are more than a congregation—you are my spiritual partners on this journey. Your faith, testimonies, and hunger for God's Word have inspired much of what is written in these pages. Thank you for walking alongside me as we navigate the wilderness seasons together.

To the mentors and leaders who have poured into my life over the years, thank you for your wisdom, correction, and encouragement. Your guidance has been instrumental in shaping my understanding of God's Word and His purposes.

To the friends and colleagues who encouraged me to put these thoughts into writing, thank you for believing in the vision and helping bring this book to life. Your prayers, feedback, and insights have made this project stronger and more impactful.

Lastly, to the readers of this book, thank you for allowing me to share in your spiritual journey. My prayer is that these words will encourage, strengthen, and guide you as you navigate the wilderness seasons of life and embrace the glory that awaits you on the other side.

With a heart full of gratitude,

Rev. Paulin Kamuangu
G.O & Senior Pastor,
Spirit Chapel Ministries

DEDICATION

This book is lovingly dedicated to the incredible people who have played pivotal roles in shaping my journey, both in life and faith:

To my father, **Rigobert Kamizelo Kamuangu**, and my mother, **Sona Palata**, whose love, sacrifices, and prayers have been the foundation of my life. Your unwavering support has nurtured me into the person I am today.

To my **brothers and sisters**, for your constant support, encouragement, and brotherly love, which have always inspired and strengthened me on my journey.

To **Rev. Prof Joshua Giasuma Kamuangu**, **PhD** and **Mrs Anny Kamuangu,** who not only brought me to Christ but also invested in my education and spiritual growth. Your mentorship laid the cornerstone of my faith and ministry. I am forever grateful.

To **Pastor Crispin Milele**, Founder of **PRAISE MINISTRIES USA**, a dedicated preacher of salvation through God's Word and Prayer Fire, for his invaluable guidance and mentorship in the ministry.

To **Rev. Dr. Ngalasi Kurisini Aggrey**, my spiritual father, who saw God's call upon my life and ordained me as a pastor. Your guidance and wisdom have been a beacon of light during my spiritual walk.

To **Apostle Ben Akotey**, Founder of Praise Tabernacle Worship Church, where I had the privilege of serving and growing for eight transformative years. Your leadership and dedication to the Kingdom were instrumental in refining my calling.

To **Pastor Chris Oyakhilome**, Senior Pastor of Christ Embassy, whose prophetic prayer in 2013 declared a new season for my life, ending my wilderness journey and ushering in God's promises.

To my beloved wife, **Ruth Kamuangu**, and our wonderful children, **Charis Kamuangu** and **Talya Kamuangu**. You are my greatest treasures, my constant joy, and my source of strength. Your love and faith in me have inspired every word of this book.

Finally, this book is dedicated to all who are navigating their own wilderness journey. May the lessons and truths within these pages guide you to discover the fullness of God's glory and the destiny He has prepared for you.

With love and gratitude,

Pastor Paulin Kamuangu

INTRODUCTION

The first truth we must grasp is this: every historical account recorded in the Old Testament is a prophetic blueprint, a reflection of the spiritual journey for every child of God. In the grand narrative of our faith, Egypt represents bondage, Pharaoh symbolizes oppression, and the Israelites enslaved in Egypt mirror the state of every soul created by God yet entangled in the world. To "come out of Egypt" signifies salvation; crossing the Red Sea is a vivid symbol of baptism by the Spirit. And just as Jesus was led into the wilderness after His baptism under John's ministry, so too is every believer called to the wilderness as part of God's divine design.

THIS WILDERNESS JOURNEY is not optional—it is essential. It is not a path we choose of our own accord, but one into which the Spirit of God leads us. Scripture declares:

"At once the Spirit sent Him out into the wilderness, and He was in the wilderness forty days, being tempted by Satan." (Mark 1:12-13)

The Spirit knows how to use the circumstances of life to guide us into this sacred space. The wilderness is not a place where your life is destroyed; rather, it is the place where your self-will, your ambitions, and your earthly desires are dismantled. When you emerge from the wilderness, you do so carrying God's will instead of your own, His plans instead of your own agenda.

This journey is profound, for it reveals a deeper truth: choosing good over evil is one thing, but choosing God over good is a higher calling. Through the wilderness, God calls you to surrender even the good you hold dear in exchange for His perfect will. This is the path to true glory, and it is the path we will uncover together in this book.

This is why coming out of Egypt is entirely different from coming out of the wilderness. To come out of Egypt is to be delivered from sin—it is the place of salvation where Pharaoh, representing sin, no longer holds you captive. Moses serves as a prophetic image of Jesus, the one sent to free us. Just as Moses was commissioned to confront

Pharaoh and lead the Israelites out of bondage, Jesus was sent into the world to deliver us from the grip of sin.

The parallels are profound:

- The world represents Egypt.
- Sin represents Pharaoh.
- Moses represents Jesus.

The children of Israel represent all humanity, created by God.

The moment you receive salvation, you are free from Egypt—delivered from sin and set apart for God. But here is the deeper truth: it is not enough to be free from sin; you must also be freed from self. The wilderness is where God leads you for this crucial work of deliverance.

Understand this: the greatest barrier to entering the promised land is not sin but self. Sin is evil, but self is the subtle enemy—your desires, plans, and ambitions that are not aligned with God's will. Not everything that is morally right is spiritually right. For example, relocating from the United States to the United Kingdom may seem like a good and harmless decision, but if it is not God's will for you, it becomes a diversion from His purpose.

The wilderness is where God deals with the self. It is not about breaking the chains of sin—that work is already done through salvation. The wilderness is where God brings you to the end of yourself. It is where He dismantles your self-will so completely that you can truly declare, "It is no longer I who live, but Christ lives in me" (Galatians 2:20).

In the wilderness, God refines you. He strips away everything that is good in your eyes but not aligned with His divine plan. This is the sacred work of the wilderness journey: the deliverance not just from sin, but from self, so that you can step fully into the promises of God.

"I have been crucified with Christ; it is no longer I who live, but Christ lives in me; and the life which I now live in the flesh I live by faith in the Son of God, who loved me and gave Himself for me." (Galatians 2:20)

Why is this truth so vital? Because in the wilderness, you must die to self. The version of you that emerged from Egypt—the old mindset, desires, ambitions, and will—cannot enter the Promised Land. In the journey of the Israelites, every individual who came out of Egypt perished in the wilderness. It was an entirely new generation, birthed in the wilderness, that crossed into the Promised Land.

So it is with you. The person you were when you left the world must die in the wilderness. Your old mindset, beliefs, and self-centered desires must be surrendered and replaced by a new creation, born of the Spirit. Do not view your wilderness season as evidence of God's disfavor, even when His promises seem delayed or life feels like a constant struggle. The wilderness is not a place of rejection; it is a place of refinement. God loves you deeply, but there are parts of you—your self-will, self-righteousness, self-confidence, and every form of self—that must be crucified in the wilderness.

In their place, the Spirit births grace, humility, and alignment with God's will. This is where the Holy Spirit's work becomes essential. Jesus Christ came to deliver you from sin, but the Holy Spirit was sent to deliver you from self. Your exodus from Egypt marks your freedom from sin; your departure from the wilderness signifies freedom from self.

Understand this: God detests sin, but He equally detests self. For this reason, He sent His Son to conquer sin and His Spirit to conquer self, which is the flesh. As Scripture reminds us: *"For the flesh lusts against the Spirit, and the Spirit against the flesh; and these are contrary to one another, so that you do not do the things that you wish."* (Galatians 5:17)

Jesus fights the battle against sin; the Holy Spirit wages war against self. Sin is evil, but self is the counterfeit good—choices that seem moral yet diverge from God's perfect will. For example, imagine a wealthy, morally upright man proposing marriage to you, yet he is not born again. At the same time, a spiritual brother comes forward, but he lacks wealth or worldly success. Self will urge you to choose the wealthy man because it appears to be the logical, moral choice. But the Spirit compels you to discern God's will, which often contradicts human logic.

The wilderness is where this battle plays out. It is where you learn to lay down the good that is not of God in exchange for the perfect will of the Father. Here, the Spirit of the Lord teaches you to let go of self and fully embrace the life God has designed for you.

You may not realize that the brother who is born of God but poor is on a journey. He is walking through his wilderness season, moving toward his Promised Land. But because self cannot see beyond the present moment, you may choose the brother with a bright present but a dark future, ignoring the one with a dark present but a glorious future. This is the nature of self—it is short-sighted, blind to the promises of God, and rooted in the here and now.

God's plan, however, is always for the future. As He declared in His Word: *"For I know the plans I have for you, plans to prosper you and not to harm you, plans to give you a hope and a future."* (Jeremiah 29:11)

Notice that God never promises us the present. The present may be your wilderness season—a time of testing, refining, and preparation. But the future? That is the

Promised Land. God's promise is to lead you into a glorious future, not to leave you where you are.

What's the takeaway? The wilderness is not optional for those who desire greatness in God's agenda. If you long to be a vessel of honor in His hands, you must allow Him to lead you into the wilderness. This is where self is destroyed, and the Spirit births the greatness God has planned for you.

The wilderness may feel like a season of struggle, but it is not a season of failure. As children of God, we do not have *problems*—we face *challenges*. There's a difference. Problems are meant to destroy, while challenges refine and strengthen. A problem is like a plastic object thrown into fire—it melts and is consumed. But a challenge is like gold placed in fire—it endures the heat and emerges purified, more radiant and valuable than ever.

The fire itself is not the issue. What matters is what you are made of. You are an indestructible material, fashioned by God's hand. Nothing can destroy you because God is for you. Even in the wilderness, His presence is with you. Just as the pillar of fire and cloud guided the Israelites day and night, so too does God guide and protect you in your journey.

This truth is echoed in His promise: *"When you pass through the waters, I will be with you; and through the rivers, they shall not overflow you. When you walk through the fire, you shall not be burned, nor shall the flame scorch you."* (Isaiah 43:2)

Notice the key here—God never says He will remove you from the fire. Instead, He promises to be with you in it. His presence is your assurance in this season.

As you journey through this book, remember: the wilderness is not designed to destroy you but to make you. Like gold, you must pass through the fire to reveal your beauty, value, and glory. Trust in God's presence and His plan for your life, for He is faithful to see you through to your Promised Land.

Chapter One

Understanding the Wilderness

THE WILDERNESS is a recurring theme in scripture, serving as a stage for deep encounters with God, self-discovery, and transformation. It is not just a barren place but a spiritual training ground, where purpose is refined, character is developed, and intimacy with God is deepened. Many great men and women of faith walked through the wilderness on their journey to fulfilling divine purpose. In this sub chapter, we will examine two pivotal figures, Jacob and Elijah, to understand the wilderness experience better.

Jacob: Wrestling in Isolation

JACOB'S WILDERNESS was not marked by physical barrenness but by emotional and spiritual confrontation. His journey to Haran, fleeing from Esau's wrath, symbolized entering a wilderness of uncertainty and fear. Jacob's wilderness culminated in one of the most profound moments of transformation recorded in scripture—his encounter with God at Peniel.

As Jacob camped alone by the river Jabbok, his heart must have been burdened with guilt, fear, and the weight of his scheming ways. But it was in this solitude that he wrestled with a mysterious man, a divine manifestation of God.

Genesis 32:24-26 records:
"So Jacob was left alone, and a man wrestled with him till daybreak. When the man saw that he could not overpower him, he touched the socket of Jacob's hip so that his hip was wrenched as he wrestled with the man. Then the man said, 'Let me go, for it is daybreak.' But Jacob replied, 'I will not let you go unless you bless me.'"

Jacob's wrestling in the wilderness teaches us that the wilderness often confronts us with our identity. Jacob entered the wilderness as a deceiver, running from his past, but he left as Israel, the one who wrestles with God and prevails. The limp he carried afterward symbolized his dependence on God.

The lesson here is clear: the wilderness strips us of our self-reliance and forces us to confront our weaknesses and past failures. It is a place where God reshapes our identity. Like Jacob, we may enter the wilderness broken, but we leave blessed and transformed.

Elijah: Finding God in the Silence

Elijah's wilderness experience paints a vivid picture of the emotional and spiritual exhaustion that can accompany great victories. After his dramatic confrontation with the prophets of Baal on Mount Carmel (1 Kings 18), Elijah fled into the wilderness, overwhelmed by fear and despair when Jezebel threatened his life.

1 Kings 19:4 tells us:
"He came to a broom bush, sat down under it and prayed that he might die. 'I have had enough, Lord,' he said. 'Take my life; I am no better than my ancestors.'"

Elijah's wilderness was one of burnout and hopelessness. However, God met him in this broken state, not with rebuke but with provision and rest. An angel brought Elijah food and water and allowed him time to recover before instructing him to travel to Mount Horeb, where he would encounter God.

The climax of Elijah's wilderness experience came not in the dramatic but in the subtle. On Mount Horeb, God revealed Himself not through a powerful wind, earthquake, or fire, but in a gentle whisper.

1 Kings 19:12:
"After the earthquake came a fire, but the Lord was not in the fire. And after the fire came a gentle whisper."

Elijah's story teaches us that the wilderness is a place of recalibration. In his despair, Elijah expected God to act as He had before—with grandeur and spectacle. But God showed Elijah that His presence is often found in the quiet and unexpected.

This is a profound lesson for those walking through their wilderness. It is easy to expect God to show up in dramatic ways, but sometimes, His most profound work is done in the stillness. The wilderness invites us to attune our hearts to the gentle whispers of God, to rest in His provision, and to trust His timing.

The Wilderness: A Place of Separation

Both Jacob and Elijah's stories highlight another critical aspect of the wilderness: separation. Jacob was separated from his family, his possessions, and his comfort zone. Elijah fled from the crowds and the pressures of his prophetic ministry.

This separation is not meant to isolate us permanently but to create space for divine encounters. In the wilderness, distractions are stripped away, leaving us alone with God. It is in this solitude that we come face-to-face with our Creator, our calling, and our character.

Psalm 46:10 echoes this truth: *"Be still, and know that I am God."*

The wilderness forces us into stillness, where we can hear God more clearly and experience His presence more deeply.

The Wilderness: A Training Ground for Purpose

Jacob emerged from his wilderness with a new identity and the promise of a great nation. Elijah left the wilderness with renewed purpose, tasked with anointing new leaders and continuing his prophetic mission. These transformations remind us that the wilderness is not an end but a preparation for what lies ahead.

Deuteronomy 8:2-3 reminds us of the purpose of the wilderness:

"Remember how the Lord your God led you all the way in the wilderness these forty years, to humble and test you in order to know what was in your heart, whether or not you would keep his commands. He humbled you, causing you to hunger and then feeding you with manna, which neither you nor your ancestors had known, to teach you that man does not live on bread alone but on every word that comes from the mouth of the Lord."

This passage reminds us that the wilderness is designed to humble us, test us, and prepare us to rely on God's word. It is a training ground, not a destination.

Lessons from Jacob and Elijah's Wilderness

- **Identity Transformation (Jacob):**
  The wilderness reveals our true selves and reshapes us into who God has called us to be.

- **Emotional Renewal (Elijah):**
  The wilderness is a place to process emotions and receive divine comfort and direction.
- **Separation for Intimacy:**
  The wilderness strips away distractions, creating space for a deeper connection with God.
- **Preparation for Purpose:**
  The wilderness prepares us for the promises ahead, equipping us with the humility, faith, and endurance needed to fulfill our calling.

Understanding the wilderness as a place of transformation, recalibration, and preparation can change how we approach these seasons in our lives. Instead of resisting or dreading the wilderness, we can embrace it, knowing that it is part of God's process to mold us into His image and prepare us for His purposes.

Jacob's limp and Elijah's gentle whisper remind us that the wilderness leaves its mark, but it is a mark of grace, growth, and glory. The wilderness is not a punishment but an opportunity to encounter God in profound and life-changing ways.

The Wilderness is Not the End

ONE OF THE GREATEST DECEPTIONS the enemy sows in seasons of hardship is that the wilderness is the final chapter of your story. He will whisper that the pain, confusion, and silence are all there is to life. He wants you to believe that your dreams are dead, that God has forgotten you, and that there is no way forward. Yet, nothing could be further from the truth. The wilderness is not the end; it is a critical part of the process that leads to God's promises being fulfilled in your life.

Think about this: before every significant move of God, there is often a wilderness. It's the divine training ground where He refines and equips you for the next stage of your journey. The wilderness is a place of preparation, not a permanent destination. If you're walking through a wilderness season right now, remember this truth—**you're just passing through.**

The Purpose of the Wilderness

Let's take a moment to understand the wilderness from God's perspective. To us, it feels like a place of delay, deprivation, and difficulty. To God, however, the wilderness is a classroom where His people learn the lessons they'll need for their future. It's a place where trust is built, faith is strengthened, and character is shaped.

The Israelites' journey is a perfect example. After delivering them from Egypt, God didn't take them straight to the Promised Land. Instead, He led them through the wilderness. Deuteronomy 8:2 explains why:

"And you shall remember that the Lord your God led you all the way these forty years in the wilderness, to humble you and test you, to know what was in your heart, whether you would keep His commandments or not."

God wasn't punishing them; He was preparing them. In Egypt, they had been slaves. They needed time in the wilderness to learn how to walk as a free people, to depend on God, and to obey His voice. Without this preparation, they wouldn't have been able to steward the blessings of the Promised Land.

This is true for you as well. The wilderness season is not wasted. It's where God strips away the old mindsets, habits, and dependencies that can't go with you into your next season. It's where He humbles you and helps you see that every victory and every blessing will come from Him alone.

The Wilderness is a Season, Not a Destination

One of the greatest mistakes we make in the wilderness is treating it like a permanent situation instead of a temporary season. The Bible is clear that there is a time and purpose for every season under heaven (Ecclesiastes 3:1). The wilderness is no different—it has a beginning and an end.

Consider this: no one stays in the wilderness forever. Joseph's time in the pit and the prison didn't last forever. David's years of running from Saul eventually came to an end. Even Jesus' forty days in the wilderness were temporary. And the same is true for you.

The wilderness is not a punishment; it's a process. And like every process, it has an expiration date. When God has accomplished what He set out to do in your wilderness, He will bring you out.

This truth is beautifully captured in 1 Peter 5:10: *"But may the God of all grace, who called us to His eternal glory by Christ Jesus, after you have suffered a while, perfect, establish, strengthen, and settle you."*

Notice the phrase *"after you have suffered a while."* The suffering has a time limit. It's not eternal. And once it has accomplished its purpose, God will perfect, establish, and settle you.

Your Journey is Not Over

If you're in the wilderness right now, let me encourage you with this: your journey is not over. The wilderness is not the final chapter of your story. It's simply a detour on the way to your destiny.

Think about Joseph. When he dreamed of leadership and authority, he never imagined the path to that dream would take him through betrayal, slavery, and imprisonment. But every step of that wilderness journey was preparing him for the day he would stand before Pharaoh and save an entire nation.

Or consider David. Anointed as king while still a shepherd boy, David spent years running for his life in the wilderness, hiding in caves and enduring hardship. But those years were not wasted. They were a time of preparation for the throne.

Even Jesus had a wilderness experience. Immediately after His baptism, the Holy Spirit led Him into the wilderness to be tempted by the devil. It was there, in a place of isolation and testing, that Jesus prepared for His public ministry.

What's the common thread in all these stories? The wilderness was never the end—it was the beginning of something greater.

Keep Your Eyes on the Promise

What kept Joseph, David, and Jesus moving forward through their wilderness seasons? It was the understanding that the wilderness was temporary and that there was something greater waiting on the other side.

The same is true for you. To make it through the wilderness, you must fix your eyes on the promise ahead. Hebrews 12:2 gives us the perfect example:

"Looking unto Jesus, the author and finisher of our faith, who for the joy that was set before Him endured the cross, despising the shame, and has sat down at the right hand of the throne of God."

Jesus endured the suffering of the cross because He kept His focus on the joy and glory that were ahead. You must do the same. Don't get stuck focusing on the pain, frustration, or uncertainty of the wilderness. Instead, lift your eyes to the promises of God.

Don't Let the Wilderness Define You

Another danger of the wilderness is letting it define you. It's easy to start identifying yourself by your circumstances, to see yourself as someone who is stuck, abandoned, or forgotten. But that's not who you are.

You are not defined by the wilderness—you are defined by the God who is leading you through it. Remember, the Israelites were God's chosen people even in the wilderness. Joseph was still a dreamer even in the prison. David was still a king even in the cave. And you are still God's beloved child, even in the midst of your wilderness.

Focus on What You're Learning

Finally, as you walk through the wilderness, focus on what God is teaching you. Every lesson He imparts during this season is vital for your future. The Israelites received the law in the wilderness, which was their guide for living in the Promised Land.

In the same way, God will give you wisdom, instructions, and revelations during your wilderness season that will prepare you for what's ahead. Write them down. Meditate on them. And when you come out of the wilderness, don't forget them.

Joshua 1:8 reminds us:
"This Book of the Law shall not depart from your mouth, but you shall meditate in it day and night, that you may observe to do according to all that is written in it. For then you will make your way prosperous, and then you will have good success."

The Best is Yet to Come

The wilderness is not the end. It's a season of preparation for the promises of God in your life. So, hold on to hope. Trust in His timing. Keep moving forward. And know that the best is yet to come.

As you walk through this season, remember:

- The wilderness has a purpose.
- The wilderness is temporary.
- The wilderness is preparing you for something greater.

And most importantly, the wilderness is not the end. It's just the beginning of the incredible story God is writing in your life.

Waiting for God's Timing

THE CONCEPT OF WAITING for God's timing is woven intricately through the fabric of Scripture. It's a journey that often challenges our faith and patience but leads to a profound revelation of God's purpose and glory. One story that beautifully illustrates this is Mary, the mother of Jesus—a woman whose life was profoundly marked by waiting, trust, and submission to divine timing.

The Journey of Mary: A Life Aligned with Divine Timing

Mary's journey begins with an extraordinary moment—her encounter with the angel Gabriel, who announces her divine calling to bear the Messiah. Imagine being a young girl, perhaps in her early teens, receiving such an overwhelming message. Yet, her response was profound: *"Behold the maidservant of the Lord! Let it be to me according to your word."* (Luke 1:38)

Mary's journey teaches us an essential truth about waiting for God's timing: it begins with surrender. She didn't demand a detailed plan or timeline; instead, she trusted God's Word, even when it disrupted her plans and placed her in a position of potential public ridicule.

The waiting didn't end with Gabriel's visit. Throughout her life, Mary had to wait for the full realization of God's promise. She waited during her pregnancy, knowing she carried the Savior but living with the humility of ordinary circumstances. She waited as Jesus grew, witnessing His wisdom and divinity unfold, and she waited at the cross, watching Him endure suffering and death. Mary's waiting culminated in the joy of the resurrection, fulfilling God's promise of salvation.

The Purpose of Waiting

Waiting for God's timing often feels like walking through a wilderness, where clarity is scarce, and patience is stretched. However, Scripture reveals that this waiting is neither arbitrary nor wasted. It's a divine process designed to refine, prepare, and align us with God's greater purpose.

In Mary's case, her waiting was preparation for a role that transcended human understanding. Her patience allowed her to witness the unfolding of prophecy and to become a part of God's redemptive plan. Similarly, our waiting seasons often prepare us for roles and responsibilities that we cannot yet fathom.

Consider these purposes of waiting in God's timing:

- **Strengthening Faith**: Waiting forces us to trust God beyond what we can see or understand. Mary trusted God even when her circumstances seemed contradictory to the promise.
- **Building Character**: Waiting cultivates humility, patience, and endurance. It's a process of shaping us into vessels capable of carrying the weight of God's blessings.
- **Aligning with God's Will**: Often, waiting aligns our hearts with God's timing and purifies our motives, ensuring we are ready to handle what He has in store.

Lessons from Elijah: The Patience of the Prophet

Another striking example of waiting for God's timing is the prophet Elijah. Elijah had moments of great triumph, such as calling down fire from heaven to defeat the prophets of Baal (1 Kings 18:36-39). Yet, he also experienced a season of waiting in the wilderness.

After the dramatic victory at Mount Carmel, Elijah fled from Queen Jezebel's threats and found himself in a wilderness, sitting under a broom tree, despondent and ready to give up (1 Kings 19:3-4). This period of isolation was not punishment but preparation.

God provided for Elijah in the wilderness—sending an angel with food and water and leading him to Mount Horeb. There, Elijah waited for a divine encounter, not in the mighty wind, earthquake, or fire, but in a still small voice (1 Kings 19:11-12).

Elijah's story reminds us that waiting is often a place of divine provision and revelation. Like Elijah, we must learn to quiet our hearts and listen for God's still, small voice.

The Challenge of Waiting

Waiting for God's timing is rarely comfortable. It requires surrendering control and enduring periods of uncertainty. You may feel forgotten, as though nothing is happening, but God's Word assures us otherwise: *"For the vision is yet for an appointed time; But at the end it will speak, and it will not lie. Though it tarries, wait for it; Because it will surely come, It will not tarry."* (Habakkuk 2:3)

The challenge lies in maintaining faith when the waiting seems endless. This is where Mary and Elijah's stories offer encouragement:

Mary's faith never wavered, even as she waited decades to see the fulfillment of God's promise in her son.

Elijah, despite his despair, waited and encountered God in a transformative way.

Both individuals trusted that God's timing was perfect, even when it didn't align with their expectations.

How to Wait Actively

Waiting for God's timing doesn't mean passivity. It's a call to active trust and obedience. Here are practical steps to wait faithfully:

Pray Without Ceasing: Maintain a constant dialogue with God. Share your fears, doubts, and hopes, and allow Him to guide you through the waiting.

Meditate on God's Promises: Anchor yourself in Scripture, as Mary did when she praised God with her song (Luke 1:46-55).

Serve Faithfully in the Present: Use your waiting season to serve others and grow in faith. Elijah served God even in his wilderness moments.

Surround Yourself with Encouragement: Stay connected to a community of believers who can uplift and remind you of God's faithfulness.

The Fruit of Waiting

When you wait on God's timing, you experience the fulfillment of His promises in ways that surpass your understanding. For Mary, the fruit of her waiting was not only the birth of Jesus but also the privilege of being a central figure in God's salvation story. For Elijah, the fruit was a renewed sense of purpose and the strength to continue his prophetic ministry.

God's timing is always worth the wait. His plans are infinitely better than anything we could devise on our own. As Isaiah reminds us: *"But those who wait on the Lord Shall renew their strength; They shall mount up with wings like eagles, They shall run and not be weary, They shall walk and not faint."* (Isaiah 40:31)

Waiting is not a passive or meaningless season; it is a divine invitation to grow, trust, and prepare for the glory ahead. Let Mary and Elijah's stories inspire you to wait with faith and expectancy, knowing that God's timing is perfect, and His promises never fail.

Grace in the Wilderness

THE WILDERNESS OFTEN FEELS like a harsh, barren land—a place of trials, silence, and difficulty. Yet, throughout Scripture, it is also portrayed as a place where God's grace is revealed in transformative ways. In the wilderness, grace becomes a lifeline, a source of strength, and an assurance of God's presence. To fully understand this, we can look to the stories of Peter and Naomi, whose wilderness seasons were marked by divine grace that brought restoration and renewed purpose.

Peter: Grace After Failure

Peter's wilderness season came not in a physical desert but in the soul-crushing weight of failure and regret. As one of Jesus' closest disciples, Peter was bold and zealous, often speaking and acting with unshakable confidence. Yet, on the night of Jesus' arrest, Peter faced his greatest test—and he failed.

Peter's denial of Jesus three times (Luke 22:54–62) marked a turning point in his life. The rooster crowed, just as Jesus had predicted, and Peter was overcome with guilt. He went out and wept bitterly, plunging into a personal wilderness of shame and despair.

But Peter's story didn't end in that wilderness. Jesus, in His grace, sought Peter out after His resurrection. In a tender moment by the Sea of Galilee, Jesus restored Peter:

"Simon, son of Jonah, do you love Me?" (John 21:15-17).

Three times Jesus asked this question—one for each denial—and three times Peter affirmed his love. With each response, Jesus entrusted him with a mission: to feed and care for His sheep.

This encounter is a powerful example of grace in the wilderness. Peter didn't deserve restoration; he deserved rejection. Yet, Jesus offered him grace, not only forgiving him but also reaffirming his purpose. Peter's wilderness of failure became the place where he experienced the depths of God's grace, enabling him to rise as a pillar of the early church.

Lessons from Peter's Wilderness:

- **God's Grace is Restorative**: Even in moments of failure, God's grace seeks to restore and renew.
- **Purpose Can Be Reclaimed**: Your wilderness is not the end. Just as Peter's calling was reaffirmed, God's plans for you remain steadfast.
- **Grace Prepares You for Greater Things**: Peter's experience of grace equipped him to preach boldly on Pentecost and shepherd the early church.

Naomi: Grace Amid Bitterness

NAOMI'S WILDERNESS was one of loss and bitterness. Her story, found in the book of Ruth, begins with a famine in Bethlehem that forces her family to relocate to Moab. Over time, Naomi faces devastating losses—her husband and two sons die, leaving her with nothing but grief and two Moabite daughters-in-law.

Broken and empty, Naomi decides to return to Bethlehem, expressing the depth of her despair: *"Do not call me Naomi; call me Mara, for the Almighty has dealt very bitterly with me."* (Ruth 1:20).

Naomi's name, meaning "pleasant," no longer seemed fitting. She saw herself as "Mara," meaning "bitter," convinced that her life was beyond redemption.

Yet, God's grace was already at work in Naomi's wilderness. Grace appeared in the form of Ruth, her devoted daughter-in-law, who refused to leave her side: *"Where you go, I will go; and where you stay, I will stay. Your people will be my people and your God my God."* (Ruth 1:16).

Ruth's loyalty and love were a tangible expression of God's grace, leading Naomi to a surprising season of restoration. Ruth's eventual marriage to Boaz not only provided for Naomi's needs but also brought her into the lineage of the Messiah. By the end of the story, Naomi cradles her grandson, Obed, in her arms—a sign of God's faithfulness and redemption.

Lessons from Naomi's Wilderness:

- **Grace Finds Us in Our Bitterness**: Even when we feel forgotten or empty, God's grace meets us in our pain.
- **God Uses Others to Extend Grace**: Ruth's love and commitment were instruments of grace in Naomi's life.
- **Restoration is Always Possible**: Naomi's story reminds us that God can redeem even the most broken circumstances for His glory.

The Nature of Grace in the Wilderness

Both Peter and Naomi show us that the wilderness is not a place of abandonment but a place of transformation. Grace doesn't always remove the wilderness; instead, it sustains and strengthens us through it.

Grace Sustains in Weakness:

In 2 Corinthians 12:9, God tells Paul, *"My grace is sufficient for you, for My strength is made perfect in weakness."* This truth echoes in the lives of Peter and Naomi. Grace sustained Peter in his failure and Naomi in her grief, proving that God's strength is most evident when we are at our weakest.

Grace Restores Identity:

The wilderness often shakes our sense of identity, as it did for Peter and Naomi. Peter felt unworthy of his role as a disciple, and Naomi believed she was no longer "pleasant." Yet, grace restored their true identities as beloved children of God.

Grace Prepares for a New Season:

The wilderness is not the end; it is preparation for what lies ahead. Peter's wilderness prepared him to lead the church, and Naomi's wilderness positioned her to play a role in God's redemptive plan.

Practical Steps to Embrace Grace in the Wilderness

- **Acknowledge Your Need**: Like Peter and Naomi, admit your struggles and failures. Grace begins where pride ends.
- **Seek God's Presence**: The wilderness can feel isolating, but God's presence is always near. Spend time in prayer and Scripture to draw strength from Him.

- **Accept God's Forgiveness**: Don't let guilt or bitterness hold you captive. Embrace the forgiveness and freedom that grace offers.
- **Look for Signs of Grace**: Often, grace comes through unexpected people or circumstances—like Ruth for Naomi or Jesus' words to Peter. Stay attentive to God's hand at work.
- **Trust in Restoration**: Believe that God can and will redeem your wilderness for His glory, just as He did for Peter and Naomi.

Grace: A Constant Companion

THE WILDERNESS MAY BE A SEASON OF HARDSHIP, but it is also a season where God's grace shines brightest. Peter's story reminds us that grace restores and empowers, even after failure. Naomi's journey shows us that grace redeems and brings joy, even after loss.

No matter what your wilderness looks like, grace is your constant companion. It is the assurance that God is with you, working all things together for good (Romans 8:28). Trust that His grace is sufficient for you and that the wilderness is not the end—it is the beginning of a new chapter of restoration, purpose, and blessing.

Chapter Two

Navigating the Wilderness Experience with the Inner Man

Another truth you must also grasp is that the wilderness is not a journey of the outward man, but of the inner man. The Israelites' physical journey through the wilderness serves as a powerful shadow of our spiritual reality. God, in His wisdom, has chosen to make everything visible, yet the true wilderness is not always a physical place. You could be in the UK or anywhere else, yet find yourself in the midst of your own wilderness experience.

Everything recorded in the Old Testament holds profound spiritual significance. It is not just a historical account, but a divine blueprint for our lives. The scriptures are filled with mysteries that can only be unlocked through revelation. To truly understand them, we must approach them with spiritual insight rather than seeking a literal interpretation. Too often, we miss the deeper meaning when we attempt to apply the Old Testament stories in a purely literal sense.

THE WILDERNESS, IN THIS CONTEXT, represents more than a physical location—it is a spiritual journey. It is where the inward man, the heart and soul, undergoes transformation. As you read the stories of the Israelites, understand that their trials in the wilderness are a reflection of our own spiritual struggles, shaping us for the Promised Land God has prepared. To navigate the wilderness properly, we must focus on the inner man, for it is in the depths of our being where the greatest work of transformation takes place.

What you must understand is that the Old Testament scriptures have both a literal and a revelational interpretation. To fully grasp what God is saying, especially in light of the New Testament, you must first understand the literal meaning. Only then can you access the deeper, spiritual truths that lie beneath the surface.

When we speak of the wilderness, we are not merely referring to the physical journey through a desert as the Israelites experienced. For those born of God, the wilderness is not a journey of the outward man, but of the inward man. Your inward man represents the spiritual Israelites. Through faith, you are the seed of Abraham, and the true heirs of the promise are not the physical descendants of Abraham, but the spiritual ones. The promises of God, including His blessings, are for those who are spiritually aligned with Him.

Just as the physical Israelites were saved from Egypt, so too must your inner man be saved from the world. Just as Moses came to deliver the Israelites from bondage, Jesus came to deliver our inner man from sin. The journey of the Israelites began in the wilderness after their salvation from

Egypt, and similarly, the journey of your inner man begins after salvation from sin.

So, it is essential to recognize that the wilderness is a journey of the inner man. It has nothing to do with the physical environment of the outward man but everything to do with the spiritual condition of the inward man.

There will be places where your outward man may be comfortable, but your inward man feels uneasy. Peace and joy may be absent, and if you find yourself in a place that lacks these fruits of the Spirit—where your spirit is not at rest in right standing with God—that place is not suitable for your inner man.

Understand this: there is a part of you—the self—that is concerned only with the comfort of the outward man, even at the cost of the peace and joy of your heart. But God never designed you to sacrifice your peace of mind and joy for material gain or temporary comfort. You cannot sell your birthright for a bowl of stew.

This is why it is so crucial to discern the physical places that serve as wilderness for you and those that represent the land of promise. If you fail to understand this distinction, you may be deceived by your senses—seeing a beautiful place and calling it your Promised Land, while overlooking a difficult situation and labeling it as a wilderness. It is only by understanding the spiritual environment of your inward man that you can truly know where God is calling you to be.

A place—whether a country, town, or city—can appear beautiful to the outward man, yet be a wilderness to the inner man. Conversely, a place may seem unattractive to the outward man, yet it can be the Promised Land for the inner man. The way your outward man perceives the world is different from the way your inner man perceives it. The eyes of the inner man are the eyes of God, while the eyes of the outward man are governed by the mind and senses.

This is why, as you journey through life, it is crucial to learn not to rely on your own understanding. In all your ways, acknowledge God, and He will direct your paths.

Proverbs 3:5-6
Trust in the Lord with all your heart,
And lean not on your own understanding;
In all your ways acknowledge Him,
And He shall direct your paths.

If you do not follow this guidance, you may find yourself walking deeper into the wilderness, thinking you are finding your way out. It is not God's will for your wilderness experience to last forever, but if you continue to walk by sight instead of by faith, you can prolong your journey unnecessarily.

The Israelites' wilderness journey was prolonged by their unbelief. Unbelief is the result of moving by sight rather than walking by faith. They were sent to spy out the land, and though God had already promised it to them, they returned with a report based on what they saw—through their natural eyes. The ten spies focused on the giants in the land, seeing only obstacles, and they came back with an evil report. But Joshua and Caleb, who saw with eyes of faith, came back with a good report.

In your own wilderness, you will face many challenges and difficulties, but you must learn to see them through the lens of faith. The ten spies saw the giants and said, "We are like grasshoppers in their sight." But Joshua and Caleb acknowledged the giants, yet their faith declared, "He who is with us is greater than he who is in the world."

This is how faith works. Faith does not deny the facts, but it speaks truth to those facts. The fact may be that giants are present, but the truth is that God is greater than any giant you may face. The truth is the language of the inner man, while the facts are the language of the outward man. If you want to reach the Promised Land, you must speak the truth, not be swayed by the facts.

The fact is what you speak when you see through the eyes of man, while the truth is what you declare when you see through the eyes of God. As you journey through the wilderness, one of the most vital lessons you must learn is how to walk by faith and speak by faith, rather than relying on sight and speaking according to what you see in the natural.

A place may appear to be the Promised Land to the outward eye, but be a wilderness for the inner man. Likewise, a place may seem like a wilderness to the outward eye, but it could be the Promised Land for your spirit. The key to discerning this difference is peace. No matter how beautiful a place may be, if it does not bring you peace of mind and joy of heart, know that it is a wilderness for your soul. Conversely, no matter how unappealing a place may seem, if it brings peace and joy to your heart, it is the Promised Land for you.

The wilderness, then, is not just a physical location—it is a journey toward peace and joy. It is in the wilderness that you learn to embrace the fullness of God's blessing, which is not just material prosperity, but a prosperity that is free from sorrow. The true blessing of the Promised Land is not the riches of this world, but a rich, sorrow-free life that can only come from the Lord.

Proverbs 10:22
The blessing of the Lord makes one rich, and He adds no sorrow with it.

Satan's goal is not to prevent you from acquiring the good things of life; his mission is to ensure that you cannot enjoy them. He will not stop you from buying a comfortable bed, but he will ensure you cannot sleep in it. He will not stop you from buying delicious food, but he will rob you of your appetite. The true battle is not over riches, but over joy and peace. Satan is after the ability to steal your enjoyment of God's blessings.

You see, there are things that money can buy, and there are things that money cannot buy. The Promised Land is the place where you possess both—the material blessings and the intangible gifts of God like peace, joy, and divine protection. If you have wealth but lack peace and joy, you are still in the wilderness. The blessings that money cannot buy—peace of mind, joy in your heart—are what make the things that money can buy meaningful. Without them, even the richest possessions become vanity. But with peace and joy, the things of this world become tools to fulfill God's purpose in your life.

What matters most to your inner man is not the comfort of your outward circumstances, though comfort is certainly needed, but the peace of mind and joy of heart that your inner man experiences. These are the treasures you should seek first. This is the kingdom of God, and the scripture reveals that the kingdom—the true Promised Land in the New Testament—is not about physical sustenance like bread and milk, but about peace, joy, and righteousness in the Holy Spirit.

Romans 14:17
For the kingdom of God is not eating and drinking, but righteousness and peace and joy in the Holy Spirit.

Now, can you see the deeper meaning of **Matthew 6:33**? It says, *"But seek first the kingdom of God and His righteousness, and all these things shall be added to you."*

If the kingdom of God is about peace, joy, and righteousness in the Spirit, then seeking the kingdom first means prioritizing your inner peace, joy, and right standing with God. Once you possess these, you have truly found the kingdom, you have found the Promised Land. And seeking these blessings first requires a journey that involves the transformation of the inner man.

Just as the Israelites began their journey seeking the Promised Land, so too must we seek first the kingdom of God in our inner lives. However, just as their journey involved passing through the wilderness, so too will our journey require us to pass through a wilderness season.

The wilderness is the place where peace is absent, where joy seems far off, and spiritual blessings feel elusive. It is a dry and barren place. But the kingdom, the true Promised Land, is where you find peace, joy, and all spiritual blessings.

SO WHEN WE TALK ABOUT THE WILDERNESS, don't limit your thinking to physical poverty. You could be rich in material wealth and still be in your wilderness. Under the New Covenant, the Promised Land is not physical, and the promised blessings are not primarily material. The true blessing is spiritual.

The scripture tells us that God has already blessed us with every spiritual blessing in heavenly places in Christ Jesus. This blessing is found in your inner man, where peace and joy abound, where righteousness flows, and where the fullness of God's spiritual gifts are available to you.

Ephesians 1:3
Blessed be the God and Father of our Lord Jesus Christ, who has blessed us with every spiritual blessing in the heavenly places in Christ.

Take note of two important things in this scripture:

- **The nature of the blessing — it is spiritual.**
- **The location of the blessing** — it is in heavenly places.

In the Old Covenant, the blessing of the Promised Land was described as a land flowing with milk and honey, and its location was physical. But under the New Covenant, the true Promised Land is spiritual, and the blessings are located in the heavenly realm. This means that you can be materially wealthy and still find yourself in the wilderness. Wilderness, in this sense, represents a lack of spiritual blessing, a place where you are no longer in Egypt (the world), but you have yet to enter heavenly places — the true Promised Land, where spiritual blessings abound.

Now, consider this mystery: **heavenly places** are not some distant, invisible realm. Heavenly places are where God is — they are where God wants you to be. Jacob experienced this on his journey. While sleeping in a certain place, he had a vision where the heavens opened, and angels were ascending and descending. He awoke and declared, *"Surely the Lord is in this place, and I did not know it. This is none other than the house of God, and this is the gate of heaven!"* (Genesis 28:16-17).

From this encounter, we see that there are places on earth that can be considered heavenly places. Jacob's realization that God was present in that specific place revealed a profound truth: wherever the Lord is, that is where heavenly places exist. If you find yourself in a place where God is not leading you, no matter how outwardly beautiful or prosperous, it is still a wilderness for your inner man.

Genesis 28:16-17
Then Jacob awoke from his sleep and said, "Surely the Lord is in this place, and I did not know it." And he was afraid and said, "How awesome is this place! This is none other than the house of God, and this is the gate of heaven!"

The wilderness, then, is not defined by your physical surroundings but by whether or not you are where God wants you to be. If you are where God is calling you to be, no matter the outward circumstances, you are in heavenly places — and you are walking in the fullness of God's spiritual blessings.

The heavenly places, full of spiritual blessings, are not just a reality after this life — they are meant to be experienced right now, in the place where God wants you to be. When you dwell where God wants you to dwell, that is where you begin to experience all spiritual blessings. These blessings are beyond material wealth; they are things that money can't buy, yet they often attract the blessings that money can buy.

These spiritual blessings include:

- Peace of mind
- Joy of heart
- Divine security
- Right standing with God through faith

Grace in every area of life, leading to all-around blessing

Such blessings are not tainted by sorrow. The blessing of the Lord makes you rich without adding sorrow to it. Once wealth is accompanied by sorrow, it is not the blessing of the Lord, because God's blessings always bring peace and joy alongside prosperity.

The true blessing of the Lord, which makes one rich without sorrow, can only be found in the heavenly places — the New Testament Promised Land. This blessing is spiritual, not material.

Remember this: the journey from wilderness to the Promised Land is a journey of the inner man. The Promised Land is not just a place of physical abundance; it is the environment that God has designed for your inner man, right here on earth. There are places in life where, despite having everything outwardly that makes life comfortable, you may lose peace and joy. Your heart may become full of worry and fear, making it clear that, though your surroundings appear ideal, they are not the right environment for your inner man.

So, I write to you, oh rich man: **you can be rich and still be in the wilderness.** The proof of being in the New Testament Promised Land is not material wealth, but spiritual blessings.

Proverbs 10:22
The blessing of the Lord makes one rich, and He adds no sorrow with it.

The Strength of the Inner Man

IN THE BEGINNING of this chapter, we established that the journey through the wilderness of life is one undertaken by the **inner man**. Now, we must understand the means by which the inner man navigates this journey—**spiritual strength**. Just as physical strength is essential for a physical journey, spiritual strength is vital for the spiritual journey.

Strength: Designed for Walking, Not Working

By divine design, strength is given to humanity to **walk**—not to work. God's intention was never for us to toil with our physical strength to achieve purpose. Instead, we were created to work through **grace**, **gifts**, **talents**, and **skills**.

Grace operates by the energy of the Spirit.

Talents function through the energy of the mind.

Skills rely on the energy of the brain.

When effort is driven by the energy of the body, it becomes laborious—a state linked to the curse placed upon Adam:

"In the sweat of your face you shall eat bread..."
—Genesis 3:19

THIS CURSE REDUCED WORK TO TOIL, requiring sweat and physical exertion for survival. However, Christ has redeemed us from every curse. For those born of God, work should no longer rely on physical strength but on the **energy of the Spirit**, which empowers us to fulfill divine purpose.

The Role of Spiritual Strength

PHYSICAL STRENGTH requires sustenance from food; without it, the body weakens. Similarly, spiritual strength requires sustenance from the **bread of life**—the Word of God. It is through this spiritual nourishment that we receive the strength to walk the journey of the inner man.

When we work with spiritual strength:

We operate in grace, enabling us to achieve what human effort alone cannot.

We transcend the limitations of physical effort, moving into a realm where divine assistance becomes the driving force behind our actions.

To function effectively in the wilderness, you must learn to lean on this spiritual strength, which sustains your inner man and aligns you with God's purpose.

God provided manna for the Israelites in the wilderness to sustain their strength for the journey, and the scriptures reveal that this manna symbolizes the word of God.

Deuteronomy 8:3 says:
"So He humbled you, allowed you to hunger, and fed you with manna which you did not know nor did your fathers know, that He might make you know that man shall not live by bread alone; but man lives by every word that proceeds from the mouth of the Lord."

This verse clarifies that the manna was not just physical sustenance but a picture of the spiritual sustenance we derive from God's word. It teaches that in this kingdom, life is not sustained by bread alone but by the word of God. In the wilderness journey of life, the strength of the inner man is sustained by this "spiritual manna"—the word of God. Without the word nourishing your inner man, strength diminishes, and the journey becomes unbearable.

In seasons of wilderness, **the manna you need is the word of God, proceeding from His mouth.** That's why it is essential to seek after shepherds who have the word of God and can deliver it to you. These shepherds, as described in Jeremiah 3:15, are those God gives according to His heart: **"And I will give you shepherds according to My heart, who will feed you with knowledge and understanding."**

These shepherds act as God-sent messengers in your wilderness, supplying your soul with the manna of knowledge and understanding through their teachings, sermons, and spiritual materials. This is one of the roles this book serves—to feed your inner man with the word of God so you can find strength for the journey ahead.

It is not just about surviving; it is about drawing joy and peace from the revelation of God's word. This joy becomes your source of strength, as noted in Nehemiah 8:10: **"Do not sorrow, for the joy of the Lord is your strength."**

The light from scripture and sermons that inspire hope brings this joy. Even in the wilderness, where joy and peace are often scarce, something must supply these essentials for the inner man to keep walking. Sorrow must be actively avoided during this season, as the scripture warns in Proverbs 17:22: **"A merry heart does good, like medicine, but a broken spirit dries the bones."**

To avoid a broken spirit, you must intentionally nourish your inner man with spiritual resources that bring peace and hope. This is the only way to maintain strength and joy as you walk through your wilderness.

There is a strong tendency to experience a broken spirit during the wilderness season. Yet, one truth stands firm—you can only survive such a season by the word of God.

Nothing else will bring joy to your heart during this time. The wilderness often feels like a season when nothing seems to work outwardly, but **everything is working inwardly.** This is because the wilderness is the place where God prepares you for what He has prepared for you. It doesn't take God much time to prepare His blessings for you, but it takes Him time to prepare you for those blessings.

This preparation is a process—a necessary one to remove the self-centeredness within you. And no process comes with speed. While the results of the process may arrive suddenly, the process itself is slow and deliberate. It's natural to feel sorrow and sadness in such seasons, but one thing must remain constant: **you must draw strength from every word that proceeds from the mouth of God.**

This word of God is the living bread that sustains your inner man. Sit with messages, sermons, and spiritual materials from men of God who have been sent to feed your inner man during this season. However, it is also important to understand the kind of word you need at this time. Look for:

- Words that edify your spirit,
- Words that comfort you in your affliction,
- Words that ignite your passion for God, and
- Words that offer hope for your journey.

Avoid teachings that condemn or suggest that you alone are the cause of your struggles. Instead, focus on words that open your eyes to God's promises, giving you hope to move forward. **Hope is essential for this journey.** Without hope, weariness and sorrow will overwhelm your mind.

In every journey, hope is your driving force. Just as faith sustains life, **hope keeps you moving.** Scripture reveals that "the righteous shall live by faith," which is the reality of our spiritual existence. But while faith gives us life, **hope propels our progress.**

These are the eternal principles of our walk with God:

- We relate to others by love,
- We live by faith,
- We move by hope.

As 1 Corinthians 13:13 declares:
"And now abide faith, hope, love, these three; but the greatest of these is love."

These three virtues are the foundation of spiritual endurance, and each plays a vital role in navigating your wilderness season.

And these three elements—**faith, hope, and love**—are essential for walking through this journey. The revelation of **God's love** must fill your heart. This revelation assures you that God is fully aware of everything you are going through and reminds you that His ultimate plan is to give you a bright and glorious future.

Think of it like a father training his son to become a soldier. The father might allow the son to endure hardship during training, knowing it is for his development and success. Similarly, every challenge you face is part of God's process of making you stronger and better equipped for His purpose. **The understanding of God's love is the first source of joy and strength in your journey.**

The second revelation that sustains you is the knowledge of **what Christ has done.** Everything God is going to bless you with comes through Christ's sacrifice. God blesses you, not because you are qualified, but because **Christ is qualified.** Christ's righteousness has been imputed to you, and God's blessings are now freely available because of what Jesus accomplished.

Romans 1:17 affirms this truth:
"For in it the righteousness of God is revealed from faith to faith; as it is written, 'The just shall live by faith.'"

The righteousness of God is the foundation for your faith. It reveals what God has already done through Christ to make His blessings freely available to you. Knowing that His blessings are based on Christ's finished work, and not on your own efforts, builds unshakable faith.

Romans 8:32 reinforces this promise:
"He who did not spare His own Son, but delivered Him up for us all, how shall He not with Him also freely give us all things?"

Your qualification to receive God's blessings lies in having Christ. When you have the Son, you become a son. In God's kingdom, **you become what you have.** If you have the righteousness of God, you automatically become the righteousness of God.

As 2 Corinthians 5:21 explains:
"For He made Him who knew no sin to be sin for us, that we might become the righteousness of God in Him."

Notice the wording here: it does not say you will *have* the righteousness of God; it says you will *become* the righteousness of God. This means God blesses you based on **who you are in Christ,** not based on what you do. Knowing this—that God is committed to blessing you even through the trials of life—will strengthen your faith.

Finally, the knowledge of **God's promises** for your life gives you hope. Faith allows you to trust in God's righteousness, but hope enables you to persevere through the wilderness, looking forward to the fulfillment of His promises.

All of this flows from **the revelation of God's Word.** Without feeding your inner man with spiritual manna, you cannot survive the wilderness season. You must understand the spiritual sustenance your inner man needs to thrive.

Walking in Obedience to God's Word

OBEDIENCE TO GOD'S WORD is the cornerstone of a meaningful and fruitful relationship with Him. It is in obedience that we align ourselves with His will, unlocking His promises and walking in His divine purpose. Obedience is not always easy—especially in the wilderness seasons of life—but it is always rewarding. To grasp the full weight of walking in obedience, we can look to the lives of individuals like Abraham and Jonah, who experienced vastly different outcomes based on their responses to God's call.

Abraham: The Blessing of Obedience

Abraham's story is one of unwavering obedience, even when God's instructions seemed incomprehensible. In Genesis 12:1–4, God calls Abraham to leave his country, his people, and his father's household to go to a land He would show him. This command came without detailed directions or a clear roadmap. Yet, Abraham obeyed.

"So Abram went, as the Lord had told him" (Genesis 12:4).

Abraham's obedience did not come without challenges. He left behind everything familiar, embarking on a journey of faith. But his obedience positioned him to receive God's covenant blessings:

"I will make you a great nation; I will bless you and make your name great, and you shall be a blessing." (Genesis 12:2).

The pinnacle of Abraham's obedience came in Genesis 22, when God commanded him to sacrifice his son, Isaac. This test of faith was immense—Isaac was not only Abraham's beloved son but also the fulfillment of God's promise to make him the father of many nations.

Despite the emotional and spiritual weight of the command, Abraham obeyed, trusting in God's faithfulness. As Abraham raised the knife, God intervened, providing a ram in Isaac's place.

"Now I know that you fear God, since you have not withheld your son, your only son, from Me." (Genesis 22:12).

Abraham's obedience brought forth blessings not just for himself but for generations to come. Through his lineage came the nation of Israel and, ultimately, Jesus Christ, the Savior of the world.

Jonah: The Consequences of Disobedience

In contrast to Abraham, Jonah's story illustrates the cost of disobedience. When God commanded Jonah to go to Nineveh and preach against its wickedness, Jonah fled in the opposite direction, boarding a ship to Tarshish (Jonah 1:1–3).

Jonah's disobedience led to a storm so fierce that it threatened to destroy the ship. Recognizing that he was the cause of the turmoil, Jonah instructed the sailors to throw him overboard. In God's mercy, Jonah was swallowed by a great fish, where he spent three days and nights.

From the belly of the fish, Jonah prayed to God, repenting of his disobedience. God, in His grace, gave Jonah a second chance, commanding him once again to go to Nineveh. This time, Jonah obeyed, delivering God's message of judgment.

"So the people of Nineveh believed God, proclaimed a fast, and put on sackcloth, from the greatest to the least of them." (Jonah 3:5).

Jonah's initial disobedience brought chaos and danger, but his eventual obedience led to the salvation of an entire city. This story underscores the truth that while disobedience carries consequences, God's mercy always provides a pathway back to His will.

The Heart of Obedience

Walking in obedience is not merely about following rules; it is about cultivating a heart that trusts and loves God. Jesus said, *"If you love Me, keep My commandments"* (John 14:15).

Obedience stems from faith and trust in God's character. It is an acknowledgment that His ways are higher than our ways (Isaiah 55:8–9) and that His plans are for our good (Jeremiah 29:11).

Key Aspects of Walking in Obedience:

Trust in God's Sovereignty: Obedience often requires stepping out in faith, as Abraham did, trusting that God's plans are perfect even when they are unclear.

Surrender of Self: True obedience requires letting go of our own desires, preferences, and fears, aligning ourselves fully with God's will.

Consistency: Obedience is not a one-time act but a daily commitment to follow God's Word in all areas of life.

Humility: Obedience requires a posture of humility, recognizing that God's wisdom surpasses our understanding.

Practical Steps to Walk in Obedience

Know God's Word: You cannot obey what you do not know. Make studying Scripture a priority, seeking to understand God's commands and principles.

Pray for Guidance: Ask God for clarity and wisdom, especially when facing decisions that require obedience.

Act in Faith: Obedience often requires action before you see the outcome. Trust God and take the first step.

Surround Yourself with Encouragement: Build relationships with others who encourage obedience and hold you accountable.

Reflect and Repent: When you falter, turn back to God with a repentant heart, trusting in His grace to restore you.

The Blessings of Obedience

Walking in obedience brings immense spiritual rewards:

Closer Relationship with God: Obedience draws us closer to God, fostering intimacy and trust.

Peace of Mind: Knowing you are aligned with God's will brings peace, even in challenging circumstances.

Fulfillment of God's Promises: Many of God's promises are conditional upon obedience (Deuteronomy 28:1–2).

Eternal Impact: Obedience often influences others, as seen in Jonah's story, where his eventual obedience led to the repentance of Nineveh.

Living in the Power of the Holy Spirit

Obedience is not something we accomplish in our own strength. The Holy Spirit empowers us to live according to God's Word, guiding us and giving us the strength to follow His commands.

"I will put My Spirit within you and cause you to walk in My statutes, and you will keep My judgments and do them." (Ezekiel 36:27).

As we yield to the Spirit, He transforms our hearts, making obedience a natural outflow of our love for God.

Walking in obedience to God's Word may not always be easy, but it is always worth it. The wilderness seasons of life are often where obedience is tested most, but they are also where God's presence and faithfulness are revealed most powerfully. Like Abraham, trust that your obedience will lead to blessings beyond what you can imagine. And like Jonah, know that even when you falter, God's grace is sufficient to bring you back into alignment with His will.

Obedience is the path to freedom, purpose, and divine blessing. Choose to walk it wholeheartedly, knowing that

God is faithful to guide, strengthen, and reward those who trust in Him.

Chapter Three

The Training in the Wilderness

The first question many may ask is, *"Does God have to make me suffer before using me?"* This reflects a human perspective that often equates hardship with punishment. However, a spiritual perspective understands the necessity of training. It's essential to distinguish between **suffering** and **training**:

- **Suffering** is the consequence of disobedience.
- **Training** is the consequence of obedience.

THOUGH THEY MAY APPEAR SIMILAR in outward experience, their purposes differ significantly. Training is a process God uses to prepare those who accept His call, while suffering often results from rejecting His call.

When you find yourself in a challenging season, ask: *"Am I facing this because of disobedience to God's call, or because I have obeyed it?"* This distinction will help you embrace God's process and understand its purpose in your life.

The Call and Purpose

From the moment you are **born by God**, you are **called by God**. Every individual created by God is designed for a specific purpose. Your journey follows a divine sequence:

Created for a purpose: Your existence is intentional; God crafted you with a goal in mind.

Called into that purpose: Being born by God activates the call to fulfill the purpose for which you were created.

Prepared and sent for it: God equips and trains you before releasing you into your calling.

Understanding this process is vital to embracing the wilderness season.

Purpose Precedes Creation

Take note: The **purpose of a thing** predates its creation. God doesn't create and then assign a purpose. Instead, He first conceives the purpose and then creates something perfectly aligned to fulfill it.

This principle mirrors the actions of any skilled manufacturer. A manufacturer does not create a product and then decide its purpose afterward. Instead, the intended function is the driving force behind the design. In the same way:

Without purpose, there can be no creation.

The existence of a created thing confirms the existence of its purpose.

God is the ultimate Creator and the Giver of purpose. Every created being and thing exists to fulfill a divine intention. Your existence is not random; it is a deliberate act of God tied to a unique, preordained purpose.

This foundational truth sets the stage for understanding why God takes us through training. Training is not suffering; it is preparation. It aligns us with the divine purpose for which we were created and equips us to fulfill it effectively.

The book of Colossians offers profound insight into the purpose of creation, emphasizing that everything was made **by Christ and for Christ**:

Colossians 1:14-16: In whom we have redemption through His blood, the forgiveness of sins. He is the image of the invisible God, the firstborn over all creation. For by Him all things were created that are in heaven and that are on earth, visible and invisible, whether thrones or dominions or principalities or powers. All things were created through Him and for Him.

This scripture unmistakably reveals that your very existence is rooted in Christ's creative power and purpose. You were made not only **through Him** but also **for Him**, which means your life is meant to reflect and serve Christ.

Understanding that you were created for Christ is the first step, but discovering how and where to serve requires a **calling**. While we are all generically created to glorify

Him, our **specific function**—how and where we contribute to His kingdom—is revealed through the calling Christ places on our lives.

Jesus Himself highlights this truth:

John 15:16: You did not choose Me, but I chose you and appointed you that you should go and bear fruit, and that your fruit should remain, that whatever you ask the Father in My name He may give you.

This verse shows that:

God created you for a purpose—your existence is intentional.

Christ chose and anointed you for that purpose—your calling is deliberate.

The Holy Spirit prepares you for your purpose—the training process is essential.

The Holy Spirit plays a critical role in preparing you for your calling, and this preparation often involves leading you into the wilderness. The wilderness season is where you learn **obedience and alignment** with God through experiences that refine your character and deepen your dependence on Him.

Even Jesus, though the Son of God, underwent this process:

Hebrews 5:8: Though He was a Son, yet He learned obedience by the things which He suffered.

This scripture underscores an important truth: suffering in the wilderness is not random or punitive—it is purposeful. It is God's method of teaching critical lessons, shaping your character, and equipping you for His greater plans.

Training occurs when the purpose of suffering is to bring knowledge. Every challenge and trial in the wilderness serves to:

Teach you **obedience** to God's will.

Cultivate **alignment** with His plans.

Refine your understanding of your purpose in Christ.

God doesn't lead you through the wilderness to harm you but to prepare you for the calling He has placed on your life. When viewed from this perspective, the wilderness is not a place of abandonment—it is a place of divine instruction and transformation.

Hebrews 5:8 says, "Though He was a Son, yet He learned obedience by the things which He suffered."

When we reflect on this verse, it's clear that even though Jesus was the Son of God, He still had to learn obedience through suffering. This teaches us a profound truth: When God allows us to go through times of suffering, it's not without purpose. Rather, these seasons are opportunities for us to learn and grow.

The purpose of suffering, in this context, is to bring about **knowledge**—specifically, the kind of knowledge that teaches us obedience and alignment with God's will. Training, in God's eyes, often involves hardship, as He uses our experiences to shape us and refine our character.

In the wilderness or through trials, God isn't punishing us but preparing us. The suffering we face is a tool He uses to teach us deeper lessons, equipping us for the purpose He has called us to. It is through this process of learning obedience that we mature and become more aligned with God's divine purpose for our lives.

There are different types of suffering, each with its own purpose. Some suffering is meant to lead to **repentance**, some as a form of **punishment**, and others to impart **knowledge**. When God allows us to go through suffering for the purpose of learning something, it becomes a form of training.

We can see this principle in the story of the Israelites. God took them through the wilderness, and in Deuteronomy 8:3, He explains the purpose behind their suffering: *"So He humbled you, allowed you to hunger, and fed you with manna which you did not know nor did your fathers know, that He might make you know that man shall not live by bread alone; but man lives by every word that proceeds from the mouth of the Lord."*

Notice the key phrase in this scripture: **"That He might make you know."** This suffering wasn't random or without purpose. It was intentional. The Israelites were taken through this trial to learn a crucial lesson: that life doesn't depend on bread alone, but on the Word of God.

This type of suffering is called **training** because it is designed to teach us. It's the kind of suffering that comes when we have been chosen and appointed by God. Other nations, like Egypt and Babylon, did not experience this because they had not been chosen by God in the same way the Israelites were. There is suffering that follows the **call of God**, and this suffering is not the result of disobedience but the fruit of obedience and alignment with God's will.

To fulfill God's purpose, you must **become** before you can **overcome**. Training in the wilderness shapes you into the person God has called you to be. For every Christian, that is to be a soldier of Christ. As 2 Timothy 2:3 reminds us: *"You therefore must endure hardship as a good soldier of Jesus Christ."*

Being a soldier of Christ involves enduring hardship. Unfortunately, many try to avoid hardship today, but hardship is not the end goal—it's the pathway. It's the fire that refines us for the inheritance God has prepared for us. Hardship is a tool of preparation, not a punishment, but a necessary part of the training process to fulfill the assignment God has given us.

You don't seek comfort in the season of preparation, for **woe** to those who seek ease during such a time. As Amos 6:1 warns: *"Woe to you who are at ease in Zion, and trust in Mount Samaria, notable persons in the chief nation, to whom the house of Israel comes!"*

Zion is not a place of comfort; it is a place of preparation, a place of **travailing**. The scripture even says, *"As soon as Zion travailed, she gave birth."* In this season, something supernatural must be birthed within you. Do not view this time as though God has abandoned you. Though you may cry out, "God, why have You forsaken me?", remember, this suffering is a result of your calling. Like Jesus, who "learned obedience through what He suffered" (Hebrews 5:8), focus on what God is teaching you through these seasons. This is the time when the Holy Spirit will use your experiences to align you with His Word.

In the Christian walk, there are two main seasons: the season of **revelational knowledge** and the season of **experiential knowledge**. Revelational knowledge is when you grow in understanding of the Word, like a theoretical foundation. Experiential knowledge, on the other hand, is the practical application—learning through your experiences.

Some things you learn through studying the Scriptures, while others you learn through what you suffer. Even Jesus, the Word made flesh, learned things through His suffering. Hebrews 5:8 reminds us that, *"Though He was a Son, yet He learned obedience by the things which He suffered."*

If Jesus learned obedience through suffering, how can we expect to be exempt from such a process? Some say that experience is not the best teacher and that it is better to learn from the experiences of others. While knowledge gained from others' experiences can guide you in your own trials, there is no substitute for firsthand experience. To think that you can bypass your own experiences and learn purely from others' is self-deception.

It's like a soldier who believes that by reading the materials of those who have completed the training, he can bypass the actual process. This approach will not make you fit for God's purposes. Just as you must learn obedience through studying the Word, you must also learn obedience through suffering. Both are essential in God's preparation for your life and calling.

Just as you come to know God through the Scriptures, in what is called **revelational knowledge**, so also you will come to know God through **experiential knowledge**. This is why the Scripture says, *"The people who know their God shall be strong, and carry out great exploits."* (Daniel 11:32)

Notice that it says those who *know* their God will be strong and do exploits. This implies that if a Christian is not strong and not doing exploits, it is because they have not truly come to know God. Many can talk about God all day, yet their lives lack the strength and exploits the Scripture promises. Their mouths may be full of talk about God, but their lives are empty of His power. Why? Because while they may know God **theoretically**, they do not know Him **practically**. They know God **revelationally**, but not **experientially**.

When you only know God by revelation and lack experiential knowledge, your ability to live in His power is limited. You might speak about His greatness, but you will not see the possibilities embedded in Him manifest in your life. Your words will be full of Scripture, but your life will be absent of His power. The key reason is that true knowledge of God is gained through both the Word and through experience.

Revelational knowledge is knowing God through His Word, while **experiential knowledge** is coming to know God through life's circumstances. Just as the Scriptures are the written Word of God, so your life is meant to be the living epistle of God, revealing Him in action. The experiences you go through are not just challenges to endure but opportunities to learn and grow in strength. What you learn from these trials is the strength that enables you to overcome future challenges.

The reason why many faint in the day of adversity is that their strength is small. Proverbs 24:10 says, *"If you faint in the day of adversity, your strength is small."* The lack of strength often comes from not understanding the purpose of the hardships you face. The knowledge that strengthens you is formed through what you endure, and yet many run from hardship, misunderstanding that it is a vital part of God's process for their lives.

The purpose of this chapter is to help you understand why the wilderness is essential. It is part of the process that prepares you for your calling. You are created for a purpose, called into that purpose, and then prepared for it. Don't rush the process—it is for your good and your future. If you want to be a vessel of honor, you must be trained as a good soldier of Christ. As a good soldier, you must endure hardship, for the bad soldier runs from it. The training in the wilderness, though challenging, strengthens you for the calling ahead.

Chapter Four

The Temptation and Trial in the Wilderness

The wilderness is not only a place of training, but it is also a place of trial and temptation. In the previous chapter, we discussed the aspect of training, but now it's time to address the temptations that arise in the wilderness.

One fundamental truth to understand is that every training comes with an examination. Just as no school exists without training, and no training exists without examinations, so it is in the spiritual journey. Every period of training in the wilderness will eventually lead to an examination, and that examination is called temptation. Temptation is essentially a test, where you are practically evaluated for the lessons you've learned during the training.

FOR EXAMPLE, if you have been under the training of the Spirit on sexual purity, you can be certain that you will face a test in this area. The test's purpose is to reveal if the lust for sexual immorality still lurks in your heart. It's important to distinguish between the desire for sex, which is a God-given gift for the purposes of reproduction and marital intimacy, and lust, which crosses the boundary into sexual immorality, including fornication and adultery. The key point is this: whenever you undergo training, temptation will follow, and the purpose of that temptation is to prove whether you have truly learned what you were meant to learn.

Temptation is not about God discovering your weaknesses or limitations—God is all-knowing, omniscient. He knows your past, present, and future. He knows exactly what you will do and what you won't do. The reason for temptation, therefore, is not for God to know you, but for you to know yourself. Often, people don't realize what they are capable of until they face specific situations or attain certain positions. It's easy to say what you would or would not do until you are placed in positions of power, leadership, or wealth. As the saying goes, "A poor man doesn't have his own character." You don't truly know yourself until you've been tested with the very things you thought you'd never fall for. The wilderness tests your character, and temptation reveals whether you have truly been transformed by your training.

The first purpose of temptation is to help you know yourself. It's easy to think that after all the training and lessons you've gone through in the wilderness, you are ready for whatever comes your way. You might even believe that you've learned obedience fully. But until you face a specific temptation—like when the Spirit asks you to empty your bank account for a work of God—you may not realize that you still have areas in your heart that need transformation. The temptation to hold on to that money, the worry about how you will survive without it, and the struggle you face in that moment all reveal that you haven't yet fully learned obedience through suffering.

If you resist and refuse to obey, God might allow circumstances to cause you to lose the money in ways that will make you regret not following His leading. When another opportunity comes and the Spirit asks you to give again, this time you will do so willingly because you've learned the hard way that delayed obedience is disobedience. You've experienced the consequences of disobedience, and that lesson will stay with you, helping you grow in obedience moving forward.

Another crucial point is that it is only Christ who can face temptation once, pass it, and remain humble. For us, we often fail and fall into temptation multiple times before we finally rise and overcome it. This repeated cycle helps to avoid self-righteousness. The Bible tells us that the righteous may fall seven times but will rise again (Proverbs 24:16). This means that before one becomes righteous, they must fall many times. It's righteousness born out of humility.

It's dangerous to have a righteousness that is rooted in pride, which leads to self-righteousness. Many fall into this trap, boasting in their own obedience and failing to acknowledge that it is God's righteousness working through them. God allows us to face temptations relying on our own strength so we can learn that we cannot overcome on our own. It is only when we recognize our weakness and depend on God's grace that we can truly overcome. When you pass through temptation and emerge victorious, it's not by your own power—it's because God is at work in you, giving you the will and ability to follow His ways.

Philippians 2:13 reminds us that "it is God who works in you both to will and to do for His good pleasure." This is a vital lesson to learn in the season of temptation: it is only with God that all things are possible. Many of us try to face temptation on our own strength and understanding, but this is a mistake. We cannot overcome the cunning tricks of the devil by relying on our own wisdom. The enemy is too deceptive to think we can face such temptation alone.

In this season, you must learn not to depend on your own understanding or strength. You need God's wisdom and strength to withstand temptation. When you try to face temptation without God's guidance, you set yourself up for failure. Remember, it is only when God is for you and with you that nothing can stand against you.

Also, it's important to distinguish between temptation and trial. When facing temptation, it is your lust that is being tested, while in trial, it is your faith that is tested. Temptation presents you with pleasure and leads to falling or misalignment with God, while trial involves pressure and can lead to failure.

Jesus faced temptation in the wilderness, but at the cross, He faced trial. Temptation is when you're offered pleasures that may lead you to deny God, while trial is when you're confronted with difficult situations that may tempt you to give up or lose faith.

IN THE BOOK OF JAMES, we are encouraged to "count it all joy when you fall into various trials" (James 1:2) because "the testing of your faith produces patience" (James 1:3). The testing of your faith through trial builds perseverance. On the other hand, temptation tests your lust, and its purpose is to produce purity, righteousness, and humility.

One of the greatest lessons we learn through temptation and failure is humility. A person who has fallen and learned from those failures is often the most humble. The scars of failure can be a powerful reminder of God's grace and a testimony of growth. You must fail before you can truly pass and grow in character. True results in life come from humility that is born from understanding your weaknesses and relying on God's strength to overcome them.

You can clearly see the purpose of both temptation and trial. Trial is the testing of your faith, and through it, God wants to teach you patience—not only patience with life but also patience in life. Patience is what you need to endure and trust in God's timing. On the other hand, temptation is the testing of your lust, and God's purpose through temptation is to produce humility. It is through humility that you learn that no one can be holy through self-effort, no one can be righteous by self-determination—it is only by the power of the Holy Spirit.

When you rely on yourself, you turn to law, seeking ten principles to practice in order to be holy. But when you rely on the Spirit, you trust in God's grace to make you holy and righteous. It is only God at work within you, making you willing and able to do His will, that enables you to live a holy life. Without God's grace, it is impossible to do His will.

Grace is God's work in you and for you. When God is at work in you, He equips you with what you need to fulfill His purpose. To walk with God, you need patience; to work for God, you need humility. Patience is essential in walking with God because He does not work according to human calendars. To align with God's timing, you must understand that He does everything at His appointed time, not at your convenience.

The Bible shows this truth in Galatians 4:1-2: "Now I say that the heir, as long as he is a child, does not differ at all from a slave, though he is master of all, but is under guardians and stewards until the time appointed by the father." This is crucial—God's plan for your life unfolds according to His timing, not yours or anyone else's. Just because others may reach certain milestones at a certain age, it doesn't mean that is the appointed time for you. When you try to rush ahead of God's plan, you will face struggles because you failed the test of faith. You must learn to trust in His timing and embrace the season He has you in.

Impatience results when we fail the test of faith, while patience is the reward when we pass it. Patience is the ability to wait for God's timing, and it is in the wilderness where this is most powerfully learned. We must accept that everything in life happens according to God's time and chance.

Ecclesiastes 9:11 reminds us: "I returned and saw under the sun that—the race is not to the swift, nor the battle to the strong, nor bread to the wise, nor riches to men of understanding, nor favor to men of skill; but time and chance happen to them all." This verse highlights the role that time and chance play in our lives. There's a natural tendency within us to force things to happen before their appointed time. This impatience often leads to frustration. Frustration occurs when we try to rush things that should unfold in God's perfect timing. Although our desires may align with God's will, we must ask: Is it God's time?

It is only when God's will is carried out at His time that we see lasting results. When we act outside of God's timing, we face struggles instead. Many have stepped into ministry, launched businesses, or entered marriages prematurely, believing they were following God's will, but because it wasn't the right time, they are now experiencing hardship. Yes, it may be God's will, but it's crucial to recognize that His timing is just as important as His will.

The Bible teaches us to "write the vision and make it plain, that he may run who reads it" (Habakkuk 2:2), but it also says, *"though it tarries, wait for it; because it will surely come."* This implies there is an appointed time for everything. Acting before that appointed time only leads to disappointment and unnecessary struggle. To walk with God, we must learn to embrace the language of patience, for the trials we face are meant to test our faith and cultivate patience in our lives.

When the testing of your faith produces impatience, it means you have failed the test of faith. However, when it produces patience, you have passed the test because you've learned to wait for God's timing. Inheriting the promised land is indeed your focus, but the Bible teaches that we must learn from those who, through faith and patience, inherit the promises.

Hebrews 6:12 says: *"that you do not become sluggish, but imitate those who through faith and patience inherit the promises."* This passage encourages us to follow the example of those who patiently endure, like Abraham. God made a promise to Abraham and swore by Himself because there was no one greater. It was through faith and patience that Abraham obtained the promise.

Hebrews 6:15 adds: *"And so, after he had patiently endured, he obtained the promise."* This reminds us that patience is not just a virtue but a necessary element in inheriting God's promises. By faith, we please God; by patience, we walk with God. Without faith, it is impossible to please Him, and without patience, it is impossible to walk with Him.

Moreover, humility is vital in our relationship with God. **James 4:6** teaches: *"But He gives more grace. Therefore He says: 'God resists the proud, but gives grace to the humble.'"* Humility allows us to receive grace, and it is with this grace that we work for God. Without humility, we cannot receive grace; and without grace, we cannot do the work God calls us to do. The humility God desires is the understanding that it is not by our own power or righteousness that we achieve anything, but by His grace.

In Acts 3:1-13, the story of Peter and John healing the lame man at the Beautiful Gate provides profound lessons in faith, humility, and divine power. Here's a breakdown of these verses:

Acts 3:1-3: Peter and John, two of Jesus' closest disciples, went to the temple at the designated hour of prayer. At the gate called Beautiful, they encountered a man who had been lame from birth and was begging for alms. His situation represents spiritual and physical brokenness, and his position at the temple gate symbolizes a desire for help and hope.

Acts 3:4-5: When the lame man asked for alms, Peter and John fixed their eyes on him, calling him to look at them.

The man expected to receive money, but Peter was about to offer him something far greater—he would give him healing in the name of Jesus Christ.

Acts 3:6-7: Peter declared that he did not have silver or gold, but what he had—faith and the power of Jesus—he offered. Peter commanded the man to rise and walk in the name of Jesus Christ. As soon as Peter took him by the hand and lifted him, the man's feet and ankles were healed.

Acts 3:8-10: The man, now healed, leaped to his feet and walked, entering the temple with Peter and John, praising God. His actions—a leap of joy and gratitude—were a testimony of the miracle, and everyone around him was amazed because they recognized him as the man who had sat at the gate begging.

Acts 3:11-12: When the people rushed to Peter and John, filled with amazement, Peter took the opportunity to address them. He made it clear that it was not by their own power or godliness that the man was healed, but by the power of God through Jesus Christ.

Acts 3:13: Peter emphasized that it was the God of their fathers—the God of Abraham, Isaac, and Jacob—who had glorified Jesus, His Servant. He pointed out that this was the same Jesus whom the people had denied and handed over to Pilate, even when Pilate sought to release Him.

Key Lessons:

The Power of Jesus' Name: Peter's declaration that the healing happened in Jesus' name highlights the authority and power of Christ. This shows us that, while we may not have earthly riches, the spiritual power we have through Jesus is immeasurable.

Faith and Action: Peter didn't just speak about the power of Christ; he acted on it. He extended his hand to the man, giving him not just words but tangible action. This illustrates that faith without action is incomplete.

Humility in the Face of Miracles: Despite performing the miracle, Peter didn't take credit. He immediately redirected the people's attention to God, recognizing that it is God's power and grace that makes such acts of healing possible.

The Call to Repentance: In the next part of the chapter, Peter calls the people to repent for denying Jesus and to turn to Him for forgiveness, emphasizing the importance of humility and reconciliation with God.

This passage underscores the themes of divine power, the importance of faith and obedience, and the need to recognize and give glory to God for all that is accomplished.

Kindly read through those scriptures for yourself and see the fruit of humility displayed by Peter. Many only see and read through this scripture and focus on the supernatural power of God in man, but when you read through, you will also see the supernatural humility in man. After Peter performed this miracle, men began to see him as though it was by his prayer and fasting, by his sacrifice of holiness and righteousness that this happened. This is the nature of religious people. Whenever they see anyone with supernatural manifestation, they will never link the supernatural manifestation to grace. Instead, they will link it to the sacrifice of fasting that such men of God have paid, and if care is not taken, you may begin to take the glory that is due to Jesus only.

This is where many men of God fall into temptation—they accept that they paid the sacrifice of fasting for the supernatural manifestation to take place. But for Peter, the opposite is the case. Kindly see for yourself what he said:

Acts 3:12: "So when Peter saw it, he responded to the people: 'Men of Israel, why do you marvel at this? Or why look so intently at us, as though by our own power or godliness we had made this man walk?'"

This is the kind of humility that brings an increase in grace. That is why, in verse 4, the scripture begins to say, "Great grace was upon the apostles." Why? Because they understood that God only gives grace to the humble, and they knew how to position their hearts for the kind of humility that brings grace—**spiritual humility**. Moral humility, which is humility before man, does not bring grace. You can be humble before man and still be proud before God.

What God describes as pride is not acknowledging the grace of God, thinking you deserve the possibility of grace manifesting in you, and believing that you are qualified for God to use you. Such a heart, filled with pride, is resisted by God, and He looks for those who never boast in their holiness and righteousness, those who never boast in their fasting. God then places His grace in them. So, it takes **faith** to please God, **humility** to work for God, and **patience** to walk with God.

At salvation, you receive faith, and through that faith, you receive the Holy Spirit. The Holy Spirit then takes you through the wilderness to be tempted and tried. The temptation is to bring you to humility, and the trial is to bring you to patience.

With **faith** and **humility**, you obtain grace; with **faith** and **patience**, you obtain inheritance. You can see for yourself in the book of **Deuteronomy** why God said He led them through the wilderness: He did it to humble them.

Deuteronomy 8:2: "And you shall remember that the Lord your God led you all the way these forty years in the wilderness, to humble you and test you, to know what was in your heart, whether you would keep His commandments or not."

Deuteronomy 8:3: "So He humbled you, allowed you to hunger, and fed you with manna which you did not know, nor did your fathers know, that He might make you know that man shall not live by bread alone; but man lives by every word that proceeds from the mouth of the Lord."

Deuteronomy 8:14: "When your heart is lifted up, and you forget the Lord your God who brought you out of the land of Egypt, from the house of bondage..."

Deuteronomy 8:15: "Who led you through that great and terrible wilderness, in which were fiery serpents and scorpions and thirsty land where there was no water; who brought water for you out of the flinty rock..."

Deuteronomy 8:16: "Who fed you in the wilderness with manna, which your fathers did not know, that He might humble you and that He might test you, to do you good in the end..."

Deuteronomy 8:17: "Then you say in your heart, 'My power and the might of my hand have gained me this wealth.'"

Deuteronomy 8:18: "And you shall remember the Lord your God, for it is He who gives you power to get wealth, that He may establish His covenant which He swore to your fathers, as it is this day."

From this scripture, you will see that the suffering in the wilderness is meant to teach humility, and the long years are to teach patience. Until you pass the tests of humility and patience, you are not yet ripe for the promised land. So, learn quickly what you need to learn.

Mind you, the temptation you face in the wilderness is not from God. God does not tempt anyone. The temptation is from Satan, and it is through your lust, because as the scripture says, "Let no man who is tempted say he is tempted by God."

James 1:13: "Let no one say when he is tempted, 'I am tempted by God'; for God cannot be tempted by evil, nor does He Himself tempt anyone."

While God does not tempt anyone, it is important to understand that God allows Satan to tempt everyone. God was not the one who tempted Jesus in the wilderness, but as scripture says, it was the Spirit of God who led Him into the wilderness for the purpose of being tempted by Satan.

Matthew 4:1: "Then Jesus was led up by the Spirit into the wilderness to be tempted by the devil."

This means that while God does not directly tempt us, He permits temptation as part of the process of testing and refining us. It's like how a school allows examinations. The key difference between the school of the Spirit and a physical academic school is that, in an academic setting, the teacher who teaches you also marks your exam.

In the school of the Spirit, the Spirit of God is the teacher, but Satan sets the exam. When you face this spiritual test, your conscience acts as the examiner. It is through your conscience that you will know whether you have passed or failed, as it judges the outcome of your test.

Proclaiming Victory and Restoration

VICTORY AND RESTORATION are central themes in the journey of faith. They signify the fulfillment of God's promises and the tangible expression of His power to transform desolation into abundance, despair into hope, and chaos into peace. The Bible is rich with stories of victory and restoration, from the valleys of Ezekiel to the tempestuous seas calmed by Jesus. These narratives remind us that God's power is absolute, His timing is perfect, and His restoration is complete.

Ezekiel: Speaking Life into the Dry Bones

Ezekiel's vision of the valley of dry bones is one of the most compelling illustrations of restoration in Scripture. In Ezekiel 37:1–14, the prophet is brought to a valley filled with dry bones—a vivid representation of desolation, hopelessness, and death. God asks him a question that seems impossible to answer:

"Son of man, can these bones live?" (Ezekiel 37:3).

Ezekiel responds wisely, acknowledging God's sovereignty:
"O Lord God, You know."

God then commands Ezekiel to prophesy over the bones, declaring life into what seemed irredeemable. As Ezekiel obeys, the bones begin to rattle, coming together, and flesh covers them. Yet, there is no breath in them. God instructs Ezekiel to prophesy to the breath, calling the Spirit to fill them, and the once-dead bones rise up as a vast army.

This vision encapsulates the power of God's Word to restore. The dry bones represent situations in our lives that appear beyond repair—dreams that seem dead, relationships that are broken, or seasons of spiritual barrenness. Just as Ezekiel spoke God's Word over the bones, we too are called to declare God's promises over our lives, trusting in His ability to bring restoration.

The lesson here is clear: no situation is beyond God's power to restore. When we align our words with God's Word, speaking life into what seems lifeless, we position ourselves to witness miraculous transformations.

Jesus Calms the Storm: Victory Over Chaos

In Mark 4:35–41, Jesus and His disciples are crossing the Sea of Galilee when a fierce storm arises, threatening to capsize their boat. The disciples, overwhelmed by fear, wake Jesus, who is sleeping peacefully despite the chaos. They cry out, *"Teacher, do You not care that we are perishing?"*

Jesus rises and commands the wind and the waves: *"Peace, be still!"* (Mark 4:39).

Immediately, the storm ceases, and a great calm settles over the sea. Jesus then turns to His disciples and asks, *"Why are you so fearful? How is it that you have no faith?"*

This story demonstrates Jesus' authority over nature and His power to bring peace to the storms of life. The disciples' fear and doubt mirrored the human tendency to focus on the chaos rather than the Savior who stands above it.

In our own lives, storms—be they emotional, relational, or spiritual—can make us feel as though we are sinking. But Jesus' words remind us that He is in control, even when circumstances feel overwhelming. Victory begins with recognizing His presence and proclaiming His authority over the chaos.

The Power of Proclamation

Proclaiming victory and restoration is an act of faith. It is declaring God's promises even when they are not yet visible, aligning our words and thoughts with His truth. The Bible repeatedly emphasizes the power of spoken words:

Life and Death in the Tongue:
"Death and life are in the power of the tongue, and those who love it will eat its fruit." (Proverbs 18:21).

Faith Comes by Hearing:
"So then faith comes by hearing, and hearing by the word of God." (Romans 10:17).

When we proclaim God's Word, we are not just speaking into the air; we are activating faith, building our confidence in His promises, and creating an atmosphere for His power to manifest.

Restoration Through the Cross

The ultimate victory and restoration were achieved through Jesus Christ's death and resurrection. On the cross, Jesus proclaimed,
"It is finished!" (John 19:30).

These three words signaled the completion of His mission to redeem humanity, conquer sin, and restore our relationship with God. Through His sacrifice, we are restored to righteousness, peace, and eternal life.

The resurrection further demonstrates God's power to bring life out of death and hope out of despair. Just as Jesus rose victorious, we too can rise above our circumstances, walking in the fullness of His restoration.

Practical Steps to Proclaim Victory and Restoration

Speak God's Promises: Identify Scripture that aligns with your situation and declare it daily. For example:

For peace: *"And the peace of God, which surpasses all understanding, will guard your hearts and minds through Christ Jesus."* (Philippians 4:7).

For restoration: *"I will restore to you the years that the swarming locust has eaten."* (Joel 2:25).

Maintain a Heart of Gratitude: Thank God in advance for the victory and restoration, trusting in His faithfulness.

Pray Boldly: Approach God with confidence, knowing that He delights in answering prayers aligned with His will.

Surround Yourself with Encouragement: Engage with others who speak life and encourage you to stand firm in faith.

Walk in Obedience: Restoration often requires action. Follow God's leading, even when the path is uncertain.

The Role of Faith in Proclamation

PROCLAIMING VICTORY AND RESTORATION REQUIRES FAITH. Faith is not blind optimism; it is a confident assurance in God's character and promises. Hebrews 11:1 defines faith as *"the substance of things hoped for, the evidence of things not seen."*

Faith enables us to see beyond our current circumstances, trusting that God is working all things together for our good (Romans 8:28). It empowers us to speak life, even in the face of adversity, knowing that our words have the power to shape our reality according to God's will.

Victory and restoration are not just distant hopes; they are present realities in Christ. Whether you are in a valley of dry bones or a stormy sea, remember that God's power is sufficient to bring you through. Speak His Word over your life, trust in His timing, and rest in His promises.

As Ezekiel saw the dry bones rise into an army and as the disciples witnessed the storm bow to Jesus' command, you too will see God's power manifest in your life. Proclaim victory and restoration boldly, knowing that the God who has begun a good work in you will bring it to completion (Philippians 1:6).

Chapter Five

The Experience of the Promised Land

We've previously explored the experience of the wilderness, which encompasses the training, temptation, and trials faced during that journey. However, it's equally important to understand the revelation of the promises that lie ahead after you've passed through the wilderness. This vision of what is to come is crucial, as it holds the key to enduring the hardships of the wilderness with joy. Scripture reminds us that Jesus endured the cross "for the joy set ahead."

Hebrews 12:2 – "Looking unto Jesus, the author and finisher of our faith, who for the joy that was set before Him endured the cross, despising the shame, and has sat down at the right hand of the throne of God."

In other words, knowing what lies ahead can provide the strength needed to endure the challenges of today. Jesus, in His suffering, found the strength to persevere because He focused on the glory that awaited Him.

UNDERSTAND THIS CLEARLY: **God will not always show you the process you will go through, but He will reveal the destination.** Joseph, a master dreamer, only saw the glory ahead, not the painful journey he would need to take to get there. He saw the stars, the sun, and the moon bowing down to him — a vision of power and authority —

but he didn't see the betrayal, slavery, or imprisonment that would be his path to that place of glory.

This is the way God interacts with His chosen ones. If the Israelites had known the trials they would endure, they might have chosen to remain in slavery instead of pursuing the freedom and victory promised to them. They cried out for the Promised Land, imagining a place of abundance — a land flowing with milk and honey, as promised in prophecy. They held on to the vision of the promise, but they never saw the path they would need to walk to reach it.

FOR EVERY PROMISE, there is a process. **The promises are revealed through revelation, but the process is learned through experience.** We often see the promises by faith, but the process can only be understood through the journey. This is why it's said, "for the joy that is set ahead," because it is this joy that fuels us to endure the challenges of the journey. The kingdom of God is like a beautiful city with a difficult road, while the kingdom that leads to destruction is like a smooth road to a bad place. This is why many take the broad way, and only a few find the narrow path that leads to life.

The path to everything God has for you is always narrow. Run away from anything in life that promises a smooth, easy, or quick process — the end of such paths is always destruction. This is why Scripture warns us that there is a way that seems right to man, but its end is destruction. This was true for Lot, who chose a path that looked good in his eyes, only to end up in Sodom, losing everything in the end.

This is a crucial truth: don't seek a smooth road for the things God has for you. The only road ordained to lead you to the Promised Land is the wilderness. It's in the wilderness that you are trained for what lies ahead, tempted for what is ahead, and tried for what is ahead. The capacity within you determines what you can receive from God. He can give you the world if you have the capacity to handle it — but this capacity is built in the wilderness.

As your journey begins, you must learn to shift your focus from your current struggles and place it on where you're headed. What you behold is what you become. If you focus on your destination, you begin to take on the image of the glory of the Promised Land. But if you fix your gaze on your present situation, you become consumed by it.

Understand this: There is a place where you are coming from, there is a place where you are, and there is a place where you are going. Scripture tells us that the suffering of the present moment is nothing compared to the glory that lies ahead:

Romans 8:18 – "For I consider that the sufferings of this present time are not worthy to be compared with the glory which shall be revealed in us."

That glory is what you should focus on. It is the blessing and fulfillment that will follow your wilderness experience. You cannot bypass the wilderness; suffering is a part of it, as Scripture clearly tells us. But after you have suffered for a while, the God of all grace will establish, bless, and settle you:

1 Peter 5:10 – "But may the God of all grace, who called us to His eternal glory by Christ Jesus, after you have suffered a while, perfect, establish, strengthen, and settle you."

You may wonder why suffering is necessary. Why can't God bless and settle us immediately? The answer is simple: if you want to share in His glory, you must also share in His suffering.

Romans 8:17 – "And if children, then heirs—heirs of God and joint heirs with Christ, if indeed we suffer with Him, that we may also be glorified together."

I love how the NLT version expresses it:

Romans 8:17-25 – "And since we are his children, we are his heirs. In fact, together with Christ, we are heirs of God's glory. But if we are to share his glory, we must also share his suffering."

It's clear: as children of God, we are designed for inheritance. The glory we are to inherit as heirs of God is tied to our ability to share in Christ's suffering. No suffering, no glory. To avoid suffering is to avoid glory.

The road to glory always goes through the cross. No cross, no glory.

But here's the mystery: you must take your focus off the process and focus on the glory. The Bible tells us exactly where to focus:

2 Corinthians 3:18 – "But we all, with unveiled face, beholding as in a mirror the glory of the Lord, are being transformed into the same image from glory to glory, just as by the Spirit of the Lord."

The Scripture doesn't say to focus on the suffering you're going through for the Lord. Instead, it encourages you to behold the glory that follows the suffering. Yes, people will mock you for choosing the narrow path, the wilderness road. But remember this: as they mock you, the Spirit of glory is resting upon you.

1 Peter 4:14 – "If you are reproached for the name of Christ, blessed are you, for the Spirit of glory and of God rests upon you. On their part He is blasphemed, but on your part He is glorified."

Blessed are you when you are reproached for Christ's sake. This means reproach will come, but keep your eyes off the reproach and fix them on the glory attached to it. As people mock you, the Spirit of glory is resting on you. What's the key point? There is glory ahead. Let that glory ahead be your focus.

Just know, it's a journey for a season and for a reason. Everything you're going through is for your glory. Your gold is only passing through fire for the glory to be revealed. All you need to do is follow the example of Jesus. Look unto Jesus, the author and finisher of our faith, who for the joy set before Him endured the cross.

Hebrews 12:2 – "Looking unto Jesus, the author and finisher of our faith, who for the joy that was set before Him endured the cross, despising the shame, and has sat down at the right hand of the throne of God."

That cross He bore is also yours. You must carry it and follow Him. Jesus said, *"Whoever desires to come after Me, let him deny himself, take up his cross, and follow Me."* So, this is a journey with a cross—and the cross is for a season. Jesus didn't carry His cross forever; He carried it for a season, but the glory that followed is eternal. The same is true for you. Let the joy of what's ahead give you the strength to endure the present. The joy of the Lord is your strength to walk through the wilderness season.

This joy comes when the eyes of your understanding are opened to see the promise land ahead. Behind every wilderness is Egypt, and ahead of every wilderness is the Promised Land.

The Promise of Renewal

RENEWAL is one of the most powerful promises God offers to His people. It represents hope, restoration, and transformation. In moments when life feels overwhelming, and when the wilderness experience seems endless, the promise of renewal reminds us that no matter how far we've fallen, how broken we are, or how challenging the journey has been, God has the power to restore, refresh, and renew.

In the midst of life's trials, the declarations we speak over ourselves are crucial. The words we say carry weight, and when aligned with God's promises, they act as catalysts for transformation. One such powerful declaration is: **"I'm coming back from there."** These words are not just a statement of survival; they are a proclamation of victory and faith in God's ability to renew and restore.

The Power of the "Come Back from There" Declaration

The "Come Back from There" declaration serves as a rallying cry for anyone who feels trapped in a season of despair, disappointment, or failure. It is an affirmation that God's promises are greater than any setback we face. Whether we are recovering from failure, illness, financial loss, or spiritual dryness, the "Come Back from There" declaration reminds us that we can rise above our circumstances.

The Bible is full of stories where God brings people from places of devastation to renewal. His power to restore is not only a future hope, but a present reality. When we say, "I'm coming back from there," we are acknowledging that God's ability to renew us is already at work. No matter where "there" is in your life—be it failure, sin, brokenness, or discouragement—you are declaring that God is not finished with you.

Renewal through God's Word

GOD'S WORD is full of promises for renewal, and speaking those promises over our lives is vital for spiritual restoration. In Isaiah 40:31, the prophet declares: *"But those who wait on the Lord shall renew their strength; they shall mount up with wings like eagles, they shall run and not be weary, they shall walk and not faint."*

This verse speaks of a divine exchange. When we wait on God and trust His timing, He renews our strength. We move from weakness to strength, from despair to hope. It is in God's presence and through His Word that our spirits are revitalized. The "Come Back from There" declaration aligns perfectly with this promise. When we declare that we are coming back, we are proclaiming the power of God's renewing presence in our lives.

When you feel like you've reached the end of your resources, remember that God's strength never runs out. He will lift you up on wings like eagles, helping you soar above the struggles of the wilderness and into His purpose for your life.

God's Restoration: A Journey of Renewal

The process of renewal often involves a journey—one that may take time, patience, and perseverance. But God's restoration is always worth the wait.

Consider the story of Naomi in the Book of Ruth. Naomi experienced the death of her husband and two sons, leaving her in a state of deep grief and bitterness. But despite her losses, God did not leave her in her despair. Through her daughter-in-law Ruth's loyalty and God's providence, Naomi experienced a powerful renewal. Ruth, who was initially a foreigner, became part of the family's lineage, and through this, Naomi's legacy was restored.

In the midst of Naomi's pain, she could not see the full picture of God's plan for her. Yet, by the end of the book, we see that God had used her circumstances for good, bringing about the restoration of her joy, family, and even her provision. Naomi's story is a powerful reminder that our journey of renewal may not be immediately visible, but God is always at work, even in our darkest seasons.

Like Naomi, we may not see the immediate results of our declarations, but as we declare, "I'm coming back from there," we are trusting that God is working behind the scenes, orchestrating a powerful restoration. His renewal is a process, but one that always brings us closer to the fullness of His plan for our lives.

The Role of Jesus in Our Renewal

The ultimate source of renewal is found in the life, death, and resurrection of Jesus Christ. Through His sacrifice, He made a way for all things to be made new. When Jesus died on the cross, He took our brokenness, sin, and shame upon Himself, offering us the opportunity for a new life in Him.

2 Corinthians 5:17 declares: *"Therefore, if anyone is in Christ, he is a new creation; old things have passed away; behold, all things have become new."*

This is the essence of renewal—becoming a new creation in Christ. No matter how far you've strayed or how broken you feel, Jesus offers a fresh start. Through His grace, we are continually renewed and restored. The "Come Back from There" declaration finds its ultimate meaning in Jesus. When we proclaim, "I'm coming back from there," we are also proclaiming our new identity in Christ, our freedom from sin, and our access to His power to restore every area of our lives.

Jesus' life also exemplified the promise of renewal. Consider the way He responded to the death of His friend Lazarus. In John 11, after Lazarus had been in the tomb for four days, Jesus declared, *"Lazarus, come forth!"* (John 11:43). Lazarus, who was dead, was called to life again through the power of Jesus' voice. Just as Jesus spoke life into Lazarus, He speaks life into us today. No matter how dead or hopeless our circumstances may seem, Jesus has the power to call us forth into new life.

When we speak the declaration, "I'm coming back from there," we align ourselves with the truth that, just like Lazarus, we can be called forth from death into life. We don't have to remain in the tombs of our failures, regrets, or struggles. Jesus is the source of our renewal, and through Him, we can experience true restoration.

Walking in the Promise of Renewal

TO FULLY WALK in the promise of renewal, we must make the decision to believe and receive it. God's restoration does not happen automatically; it requires an active faith. We must continue to proclaim that we are coming back from our hardships and trust in God's ability to restore.

The key to experiencing the fullness of God's renewal is persistence. When the wilderness seems overwhelming, when it feels like the promise of renewal is distant, keep declaring, "I'm coming back from there." When you feel like giving up, let these words serve as a reminder that your breakthrough is on the horizon. Through faith and the power of declaration, we partner with God in His restoration work.

The journey may take time, and the process of renewal may not always be easy, but God's promise stands firm: **He is faithful to complete the work He has started in us** (Philippians 1:6). Every trial, every challenge, and every wilderness experience is an opportunity for God to show His power of renewal.

The promise of renewal is not just a distant hope; it is a present reality in Christ. When you declare, "I'm coming back from there," you are not just speaking words into the air—you are partnering with God in the process of restoration. Just as Ezekiel spoke life into dry bones, and Jesus called Lazarus from the tomb, your declarations can bring life, transformation, and renewal to every area of your life.

Embrace the power of God's Word, and speak life over your circumstances. Proclaim victory, restoration, and renewal, and trust that God, in His perfect timing, will fulfill His promise to restore all things. The wilderness is not the end; it is merely the season before your divine renewal.

Walking in Divine Victory

VICTORY is not just a destination but a way of life—a life lived in constant triumph over the challenges, adversities, and wilderness experiences that we face. As believers, we are not simply called to endure hardships; we are called to walk in divine victory, rooted in the finished work of Christ on the cross. This victory is not one we attain through our own strength, but through the power of God's grace working in us.

In our wilderness seasons, it may seem as though victory is distant, and the road to triumph is long and uncertain. But the truth is, the moment we step into relationship with Christ, we enter into a journey of victory that is guaranteed by His sacrifice and resurrection. Walking in divine victory is not a matter of wishing for it or hoping for it—it's a matter of recognizing the victory already won on our behalf and stepping into it with faith and authority.

Victory in Christ: A Finished Work

The foundation of walking in divine victory is understanding that Jesus Christ has already won the victory for us. On the cross, He defeated sin, death, and all the forces of darkness. Jesus' sacrifice was complete, and through His resurrection, He secured a victory that is now available to all who believe in Him.

In 1 Corinthians 15:57, we are told, *"But thanks be to God, who gives us the victory through our Lord Jesus Christ."* This verse makes it clear that our victory is not based on our own efforts but on what Jesus accomplished for us. We are more than conquerors through Him who loved us (Romans 8:37). This truth is powerful because it shifts our perspective from striving for victory to living in the victory that has already been won.

The victory that Christ offers is comprehensive—it touches every area of our lives, from our relationships to our finances, from our health to our emotions. It is a victory that empowers us to live above our circumstances, no matter how difficult they may seem. When we understand that victory is a gift already secured by Christ, we can stop fighting for what has already been given to us and begin to walk confidently in it.

Walking in Authority

To walk in divine victory, we must recognize and walk in the authority that has been given to us as children of God. Jesus not only secured victory for us, but He also delegated His authority to us. In Matthew 28:18, Jesus declares, *"All authority has been given to Me in heaven and on earth."* And in Luke 10:19, He gives us this authority: *"Behold, I give you the authority to trample on serpents and scorpions, and over all the power of the enemy, and nothing shall by any means hurt you."*

This authority is a vital part of walking in divine victory. It's not enough to know that we have victory in Christ—we must exercise the authority He has given us. This means standing firm against the attacks of the enemy, declaring God's promises over our lives, and refusing to allow fear, doubt, or unbelief to hold us captive.

Jesus' authority over the enemy is the same authority He has given to us. When we walk in this authority, we are no longer passive victims of our circumstances but active participants in the victory that Christ has won. We are equipped to resist the enemy's schemes, overcome obstacles, and walk confidently toward the promises God has for us.

Victory Through Faith

Faith is a key component in walking in divine victory. In 1 John 5:4, we are told, *"For whatever is born of God overcomes the world. And this is the victory that has overcome the world—our faith."* Our faith in God's promises enables us to walk in victory, even when circumstances suggest otherwise.

Faith does not ignore the reality of challenges—it acknowledges the presence of obstacles while choosing to trust in God's ability to overcome them. Faith sees beyond the immediate struggles to the greater reality of God's promises. It believes that, no matter how impossible the situation may seem, God is faithful to bring us through and give us the victory.

Walking in divine victory requires us to trust God fully. It means relying on His Word and His promises, even when our circumstances seem to contradict them. Just as the Israelites were instructed to walk around the walls of Jericho in obedience to God's command, knowing full well that the city seemed impregnable, we too must obey God's Word with unwavering faith, knowing that He will deliver victory in His perfect timing.

Victory Over the Enemy

A key aspect of walking in divine victory is recognizing that we are in a spiritual battle. The enemy seeks to steal, kill, and destroy, but through Christ, we are more than equipped to overcome. The Bible gives us numerous promises of victory over the enemy. In James 4:7, we are instructed, *"Submit yourselves therefore to God. Resist the devil, and he will flee from you."* Our victory over the enemy is assured when we stand firm in God's Word and resist his lies.

Jesus exemplified this when He was tempted by the devil in the wilderness. In Matthew 4:1-11, we see that Jesus used the Word of God to resist temptation, and the enemy fled. This same victory is available to us today. When we face temptation, discouragement, or doubt, we can resist the enemy by standing firm in God's truth. We can declare God's promises over our lives and trust that His Word is powerful enough to defeat any attack.

The key to overcoming the enemy is not relying on our own strength, but on God's power. Ephesians 6:10-11 tells us, *"Finally, be strong in the Lord and in the power of His might. Put on the whole armor of God, that you may be able to stand against the wiles of the devil."* As we put on the armor of God and rely on His strength, we walk in the victory that Jesus has already secured.

Victory in the Wilderness

Often, divine victory is not just about overcoming external battles—it's about overcoming the battles within us. The wilderness seasons in our lives are often the greatest opportunities for personal victory. In these seasons, God is refining us, strengthening us, and preparing us for the promises He has for us.

The wilderness is a place where many people lose sight of victory, feeling overwhelmed and defeated. However, the wilderness is not the end—it is part of the journey. It's in the wilderness where our faith is tested, our character is developed, and our dependence on God is strengthened. Just as the Israelites wandered in the wilderness for forty years before they entered the Promised Land, we too may find ourselves in seasons where it feels like progress is slow, and victory is far away. Yet, it is in these moments of challenge that God is doing the deep work necessary for our ultimate victory.

In the wilderness, we learn to rely on God's provision, to trust in His timing, and to declare His victory over our lives. It is in the wilderness where we discover that God's victory is not just an outward circumstance, but an inward reality that enables us to face anything with confidence and courage.

Victory in Every Season

One of the most important aspects of walking in divine victory is recognizing that victory is not only for certain seasons but for every season of our lives. Whether we are in the midst of a battle, facing a wilderness season, or enjoying a time of blessing, God's victory is always available to us.

In every situation, we can walk in the victory that comes from Christ. This doesn't mean that we won't face difficulties or challenges, but it does mean that, no matter what we go through, we are more than conquerors in Christ Jesus (Romans 8:37).

Victory is not just about the absence of struggle—it is about the presence of God's peace and power in the midst of our struggles. Walking in divine victory means knowing that God is with us, equipping us, and empowering us to overcome. We are not fighting for victory—we are fighting from a place of victory.

Walking in divine victory is a call to live in the reality of what Christ has already accomplished for us. It is recognizing that, through His sacrifice, we are more than conquerors. It is walking in the authority He has given us, resisting the enemy, and trusting in His promises by faith. Divine victory is not a distant hope—it is a present reality available to every believer. Whether in the wilderness or in times of blessing, we can walk in divine victory, confident that God is with us, for us, and empowering us to overcome every challenge we face.

Reflective Questions and Group Discussion Prompts

Reflective Questions for Individual Study:

- How has the concept of the wilderness changed your perspective on trials and challenges in your life?
- In what ways have you experienced God's grace, strength, or guidance during difficult seasons?
- Are there specific lessons or habits you've developed in your wilderness that you can carry into your promised land?
- How do you discern whether you're waiting on God or wasting time? What steps can you take to align more closely with His timing?
- What scriptures, teachings, or revelations have sustained you the most during wilderness seasons, and how can you use them to encourage others?

Group Discussion Prompts:

- Share how understanding the wilderness has helped you navigate challenges in your career, relationships, or spiritual growth.
- Discuss practical ways to draw strength from the Word of God and maintain hope and joy during trials.

- Reflect on the role of obedience in your spiritual journey. How does walking in obedience impact your wilderness experience and prepare you for victory?
- How can we, as a community, support one another in discerning God's timing and staying focused on His promises?
- Share examples of how God has brought restoration or renewal in areas of your life after a wilderness season.

Practical Call to Action

- **Reflect on Your Journey:** Take time to journal about the wilderness seasons in your life, noting the lessons learned, the growth achieved, and the ways God has shown Himself faithful.
- **Pray with Purpose:** Dedicate specific time to pray about your current season, asking God for clarity, strength, and alignment with His will. Seek His Word as daily sustenance for your inner man.

Take Action:

- Identify one area in your life where you can apply a principle from this book—be it waiting on God's timing, walking in obedience, or drawing strength from His promises.
- Memorize at least one scripture that resonates with your current journey and meditate on it daily.
- Find a trusted spiritual mentor or group to share insights from this book and encourage one another in your walks with God.

Live with Hope and Victory: Remember, the wilderness is not the end. Walk boldly in the knowledge that God's purpose for your life is greater than any trial. Stay anchored in faith, hope, and love, trusting that His promises will be fulfilled in due season.

Carry this truth with you: *God's grace is sufficient, His timing is perfect, and His strength is made perfect in your weakness. Walk in faith, knowing that your wilderness is preparing you for the victory and restoration He has promised.*

CONCLUSION

From this book, I trust you've come to understand that whatever you're experiencing, God is fully aware of it. You must be able to discern whether your suffering is a result of disobedience or if it's part of God's plan for your growth and purpose. Are you facing trials for training, refinement, or as a consequence of turning away from His will? This awareness will help you know whether you are truly waiting on God or simply wasting time. It's easy to confuse the two—waiting can feel like wasting if you're not discerning God's purpose in the moment.

ONE CLEAR INDICATOR THAT YOU'RE NOT WASTING TIME is if God is speaking to you. When God is silent in your situation, it's a sign to check your heart. If He's not acting but is still speaking, then you are indeed waiting and not wasting. The key is hearing His word consistently. The Israelites in the wilderness were sustained by the manna, which represents the word of God in our lives. So, I ask you: What is God saying to you?

Remember, if God isn't doing anything in your life, make sure He's still saying something. His word is the foundation on which you stand, and it's through His word that you know your waiting is not in vain.

Don't fall into the trap of assuming you're waiting just because things aren't progressing. It's a costly assumption to think you're in a season of waiting when you might actually be in a season of wasted opportunity. Be attentive to God's voice, for it is the guiding force that will help you navigate your wilderness toward the promises ahead.

By the grace and the Inspiration of God, we have illuminated the reality of the wilderness experience. We've explored its purpose, the training it provides, the temptations and trials it holds, and the beauty behind them. We've discussed the importance of focusing on the glory ahead as you walk through this season. This journey is about learning the lessons God wants to teach you. Make sure you are recording the lessons, day by day, as God speaks to you during this time.

Just as the Israelites received all the laws they needed to live in the Promised Land during their time in the wilderness, so too will God equip you in this season. The wilderness is not just about enduring hardship; it's about preparation for the promises ahead. As you approach the fulfillment of God's promises, remember the lessons learned and the words He has spoken to you.

The danger that comes with blessing is often greater than the danger that comes with suffering. Do not let the words God has spoken to you in your wilderness season depart from your heart. As you enter the Promised Land, you must meditate on His word day and night, so that you may prosper and succeed in all that you do.

Know this for certain: In all the training, trials, and temptations you face, none is more than you can bear. God knows your individual capacity. He will never allow you to face trials that are beyond what you can handle.

1 Corinthians 10:13 reminds us: "No temptation has overtaken you except such as is common to man; but God is faithful, who will not allow you to be tempted beyond what you are able, but with the temptation will also make the way of escape, that you may be able to bear it."

Destruction only happens when trials exceed your capacity. Rest assured, God will never allow that. So, if you are facing challenges, know that God believes in your ability to endure and emerge victorious.

Shalom!

www.ingramcontent.com/pod-product-compliance
Lightning Source LLC
Chambersburg PA
CBHW071402130526
44581CB00010B/43